# THE ENDURING RELEVANCE OF WALTER RODNEY'S HOW EUROPE UNDERDEVELOPED AFRICA

# THE ENDURING RELEVANCE OF WALTER RODNEY'S HOW EUROPE UNDERDEVELOPED AFRICA

Karim F Hirji

Daraja Press

Published by Daraja Press
http://darajapress.com
© Karim F Hirji 2017
All rights reserved.
Cover design: Base X Studio

**Library and Archives Canada Cataloguing in Publication**

Hirji, Karim F., author
The enduring relevance of Walter Rodney's 'How Europe Underdeveloped Africa' / Karim F Hirji.

Includes bibliographical references.

Issued in print and electronic formats.

ISBN 978-0-9952223-9-7 (softcover).–ISBN 978-0-9953474-0-3 (ebook)

1. Rodney, Walter. How Europe underdeveloped Africa.
2. Africa–History–20th century–Historiography.
3. Africa–History–Textbooks. I. Title.

DT19.7.R62H57 2017   960.072'2   C2016-907305-X

C2016-907306-8

To

**Rafik Hirji**
*Competent Professional*
*Compassionate Human Being*
*Brother, Like No Other*

and

**Ed Ferguson**
*Astute Historian*
*Committed to Social Justice*
*Genuine Friend*

STILL A GOOD IDEA ...

INTERVIEW WITH GANDHI, 1931:

**Interviewer:** *Mister Gandhi, what do you think of Western civilization?*
**MK Gandhi:** *I think it would be a good idea.*

ON IRAQ SANCTIONS, 12 MAY 1996:

**Lesley Stahl:** *We have heard that half a million children have died. I mean that's more children than died in Hiroshima. And, you know, is the price worth it?*
**US Secretary of State Madeleine Albright:** *I think this is a very hard choice, but the price, we think the price is worth it.*

TOWN HALL MEETING, 13 MAY 1996:

**US Secretary of State Madeleine Albright:** *If we have to use force, it is because we are America! We are the indispensable nation. We stand tall, and we look further into the future.*

# CONTENTS

| | |
|---|---:|
| *Preface* | xi |
| 1. The book | 1 |
| 2. The global context | 13 |
| 3. A grand reversal | 17 |
| 4. Rodney the revolutionary | 21 |
| 5. Rodney and historiography | 25 |
| 6. Criticisms of the book | 31 |
| 7. Rodney in the classroom | 59 |
| 8. Contemporary relevance | 77 |
| 9. Hope and struggle | 93 |
| *Photograph from the archives* | 108 |
| *Acknowledgements* | 109 |
| *Major writings of Walter Rodney* | 110 |
| *References* | 113 |
| *About the author* | 122 |

# PREFACE

This book is about a book, a book which was the 20th century's most important book on African history. I talk of Walter Rodney's preeminent, paradigm-shifting text, *How Europe Underdeveloped Africa* (*HEUA*). The primary theme developed in these pages is that *HEUA is* as relevant for Africa and beyond today, as it was when it came out 45 years ago. Its importance for understanding the continent's past and present trajectories, and the myriad of grave socio-economic problems it faces has not diminished. It is as well pivotal for formulating a viable strategy to confront these problems and embark on the path to genuine development for its people. And as we examine various aspects of his book, the life of the author is also brought into the picture, though to a secondary degree.

The voices that dominate the modern social and political landscape, though, hold otherwise: As with scores of progressive intellectuals and activists of the past, the prevailing ideology functions to relegate Rodney into the deepest, almost unreachable, ravines of memory. A person who once was widely known is now a nonentity, a stranger to the youth in Africa and the Caribbean. And when they encounter him in the classroom, it is through secondary sources that distort both what he actually wrote and his framework of historical analysis.

In addition, there is a conscious, concerted effort from some quarters to make the case that even if Rodney's ideas were pertinent for the colonial and early post-colonial African conditions, they do not hold water today. They say that it is not an external entity but Africa's power hungry and corrupt leaders who are underdeveloping the continent today.

These misguided views are based on viewing society through disjoint compartments of politics, culture, social affairs and economics. They paint a shallow picture of the relationship between the internal and the external, between economics and politics, and between growth and development. And, they derive from not appreciating the structural and class nature of the phenomenon we call 'underdevelopment.' Their flaws rest on a fundamental ideological bias: that private enterprise and 'donor assistance' constitute the indispensable saviours of Africa.

On the other hand, an integrated, dynamic, dialectical perspective of the type deployed by Rodney allows us to formulate an empirically sound and coherent picture of Africa, past and present, and chart a viable, self-guided path out of the maladies it faces. Hence I place heavy emphasis on the method of analysing history and society employed in *HEUA*.

To develop an appreciation for Rodney's method, I begin by introducing *HEUA*, and recounting its initial impact. I then portray in general terms the global scene of that era. This leads to an overview of the waves of mental liberation unleashed by progressive movements and intellectuals as a part of the struggle to change an unjust societal reality. Walter Rodney was a key figure in that process.

Yet, in the decades that followed, these phenomenal achievements were subjected to an almost total reversal. Works of many prominent progressives were erased from popular and academic memory as if the entire episode had been a dream. But a few hardy ones stood their ground. *HEUA* ranks among them.

After delving into these matters, I focus on Walter Rodney. He was not an arm chair academic but a revolutionary in the true sense of the word. And he had a decisive impact on the methodology of conceptualizing African history. Going further, I list and respond to the main criticisms of *HEUA* that have been expressed over time. And this leads me to ask: How do the current students of African history encounter Rodney? To answer this query, I critically review the representations of *HEUA* in major textbooks on the general history of Africa.

In the final two chapters, I sum up my case for the enduring relevance of Rodney and *HEUA*, and describe my personal interactions with this towering specimen of humanity. My observations become a springboard that leads me to ponder: In his wake and spirit, where do we, as African patriots, go from here?

Walter Rodney lived and died for the people. Other progressive intellectuals/activists of that era made similar sacrifices. They have left us a priceless legacy. The new generation needs to critically engage with them, to learn from their struggles, achievements and errors. I hope this book will propel that on-going but presently slow-moving process forward.

Karim Hirji<br>
January 2017

## Chapter 1

## THE BOOK

Walter Rodney's *How Europe Underdeveloped Africa* (*HEUA*) is no doubt the 20th century's most important and influential book on African history. Revolutionizing the rendition of the continent's past and present through its methodology, substance and style, its impact was felt far beyond academia. It inspired, educated and directed countless readers, young and old, from all walks of life, towards anti-imperialist, Pan-Africanist and socialistic perspectives and actions. As such, it was a potent weapon in the struggle for social liberation,

Rodney wrote *HEUA* while at the History Department of the University of Dar es Salaam. The Zanzibari revolutionary AM Babu wrote the postscript. *HEUA* was published jointly by the Tanzania Publishing House (Dar es Salaam) and Bogle-L'Ouverture Publications (London) in 1972. A North American print by the Howard University Press came out in 1974. The UK edition has had several reprints. In East Africa, it has been kept in print continuously by two local publishing houses. A year after Rodney's assassination in 1980, a new edition was issued by Howard University Press. It contained an introduction by Vincent Harding, William Strickland and Robert Hill that gave an apt overview of the life and work of the fallen hero.

*HEUA* has been translated into four languages: Portuguese (1975), German (1980), Spanish (1982) and French (1986). A Chinese translation is in the works.

In 2011, the Walter Rodney Foundation in association with Pambazuka Press, CODESRIA and Black Classic Press, Inc., brought out a new version with attractive design features. Available in both print and e-book format, it featured ringing endorsements from thirteen eminent progressive scholars and stalwarts of social justice: Samir Amin, Horace Campbell, Angela Y Davis, Bill Fletcher, Norman Girvan, Gerald Horne, Lewis R Gordon, Adam Hochschild, Amina

Mama, Adebayo Olukoshi, Issa Shivji, Cornel West and Emira Woods. The major improvement in this version was the inclusion of a detailed Index.

Considering the diversity of continental conditions, societal dimensions, and historical nuances it deals with, one cannot summarize *HEUA* in a few pages without risking oversimplification. Yet, to facilitate the ensuing discussion, that is what I attempt below. (All the quotes and page references to *HEUA* are from the 2011 edition).

*HEUA* has six chapters and a postscript.

### CHAPTER 1: SOME QUESTIONS ON DEVELOPMENT

This chapter explains the two primary concepts that underpin the book: development and underdevelopment. For human society,

> development implies an increasing capacity to regulate both internal and external relationships.

Development thereby is a multi-dimensional process, encompassing mode of life, production, health, transport, education, culture and other societal aspects. Of particular import is that Rodney does not regard development narrowly as equivalent to economic growth, especially as measured by conventional criteria like GDP and per capita income.

Underdevelopment, the other side of the coin, is:

1. Progressive loss by a society over the control of its own destiny.
2. Emergence and strengthening of structures of external dependency in the economy, health, education, culture, and state organs.
3. Net transfer of resources and economic surplus to external companies and nations through gross underpayment to producers and unfair, illicit exchange.
4. A growing gap between the dominant and dominated nations in terms of technological capacity, infrastructure, social amenities and the standard of life.
5. Consolidation of a pattern of social stratification whereby local economic and political elites benefit magnificently while the masses at the bottom experience marginal progress, at best.
6. Increasing social tensions and conflict.

Underdevelopment at its zenith is manifested by a widely-held conviction that without external 'donors' the nation would plunge into an abyss. Virtually all local intellectuals, journalists and political pundits beat their drums, sing their songs and dance to their tunes.

## CHAPTER 2: HOW AFRICA DEVELOPED BEFORE THE COMING OF THE EUROPEANS: UP TO THE 15TH CENTURY

Rodney shows that the social formations in Africa prior to the European incursion ranged from the rudimentary communal to the advanced feudal, and varied in-between forms. There were complex organizational and state structures, productive agricultural systems for food and non-food crops, expansive trade networks, elaborate transport systems, intricate state and organizational systems and an array of cultural and educational patterns. His specific examples depict a tapestry of societies where the economy, social structure, and the political and organizational order functioned in an integrated manner. Though most societies had recently emerged from communalism, a few exhibited technological capabilities approaching that of contemporary Europe.

Importantly, he observes that though slaves were present in some places, no African society had passed through the slave mode of production. Additionally, despite the prevalence of commodity production and trade networks, no African society has yet shown signs of transition to the capitalist mode of production.

## CHAPTER 3: AFRICA'S CONTRIBUTION TO EUROPEAN CAPITALIST DEVELOPMENT: THE PRE-COLONIAL PERIOD

In this chapter, which extends to the onset of direct colonial rule, Rodney describes the nature and extent of the contribution of Africa to the consolidation and flowering of technologically advanced capitalist societies in Europe. He begins by depicting development and underdevelopment as two interconnected sides of the same coin. One engenders the other; the development of Europe was consequent upon the underdevelopment of Africa, and *vice versa*.

Europe attained its initial dominance through superior armaments and ships. Unfair terms were imposed on local African populations as it traders scoured the continent for gold, other commodities and, later, slaves. In the process, African communities were devastated as European companies prospered and its economies progressed. The former also contributed to the expansion of the knowledge base of the latter.

This was not an economically linear or socially homogeneous process. Interspersed with ups and downs, it was intertwined with class and regional divisions within Europe and Africa. Ruling elements in some African communities facilitated European exploitation of neighboring peoples. Lower classes within Europe were brutalized. Rodney does not just attend to economic structures but also considers the complex nature of social relations involved in this historical process.

Rodney does not conceptualize imperialism purely in terms of race. Yet, he does not ignore or marginalize the issue of race. While economics and internal/external class relations constitute the foundation of imperialism, racism is an integral feature of imperial domination. His nuanced approach on this issue has evaded the liberals or Africanists for whom the race issue has purely binary, black/white implications.

## CHAPTER 4: EUROPE AND THE ROOTS OF AFRICAN UNDERDEVELOPMENT: UP TO 1885

In this chapter Rodney marshals evidence for the proposition that the slave trade and associated European incursions laid the foundation for the long-term underdevelopment of Africa. Entailing 'warfare, trickery, banditry, and kidnapping,' the capture and transportation of Africans resulted in the loss of millions of lives. Shipment to the Americas under horrendous conditions killed about a fifth of those placed on board. The overall population loss to Africa reached up to a hundred million.

In localities where the forcible seizure of humans was extensive and of long duration, the impact was catastrophic. While energetic, economically active women and men were taken away, the infirm, elderly and the very young were left behind. Their lives were prematurely shortened. Systems of agriculture, mining, production of metal, cotton, wood, straw, clay and leather goods, trade, transport, and governance that had evolved over centuries were significantly damaged. Inter-generational transmission of cultural practices, knowledge base and vital skills was interrupted. People lived in a perpetual state of violence, insecurity and fear. Communities that had lived in relative harmony with each other became enemies overnight.

The slave trade produced networks stretching from the coast to the interior across which slaves were captured and conveyed. Africans were pitted against one another to an historically unprecedented extent. The trade also gave rise to new forms of social and class relations and struggles in Africa that had internal as well as external roots.

Rodney lambasts historians who, pointing to the gains made by a few African groups in this nefarious trade, seek to downplay its effects. Yet, his analysis of its impact is neither simplistic nor one-sided. Other than the communities that facilitated the capture of Africans for sale, he delineates three categories of impacted areas: those which suffered the drastic impact of the sort depicted above; areas where such effects were minimal because they either managed to successfully defend themselves or were distant from the coast; and areas which prospered through internal growth or developed more effective military capacity to fight off the external threat. These societies excelled due to their own innovative organizational and economic efforts.

For the continent as a whole, the impact was profoundly negative. It placed Africa under conditions that hindered autonomous development. The bonds of dependency on Europe were entrenched. The extensive economic and trade relations between different areas of Africa were inexorably replaced by unfair trade between Africa and the Western world. Rodney draws attention to African societies where the bonds of dependency had been so firmly internalized that they actually opposed the end of the slave trade.

The slave trade ended when it was no longer consonant with the further development of capitalism. The system needed 'free' but cheap labour to enhance productivity, production, markets and profits. Slavery and its antecedents set the stage for the subsequent imposition of colonial rule. In an ironic twist of history, anti-slavery sentiment and 'civilizing the natives' became prime justifications for colonialism.

## CHAPTER 5: AFRICA'S CONTRIBUTION TO THE CAPITALIST DEVELOPMENT OF EUROPE: THE COLONIAL PERIOD

In the previous chapter, Rodney, without going into specifics, states that Africans generally resisted direct control over their lives and lands by outsiders. But that resistance was progressively crushed, often through brutal means.

Direct rule enabled the colonial powers to convert African territories into appendages providing large quantities of essential agricultural and mining inputs for their expanding industries, and an array of consumer items like tea, coffee, spices and nuts for their growing populations. The colony formed a captive market for metropolitan industries producing things like soap, matchboxes, cooking oil, shoes, cotton goods and confectionary as well as tools and materials for construction, crafts, administrative functions and transportation.

The fundamental feature of this process was that Africans were at a distinct disadvantage compared to the managers and governmental officials from the metropolis. In all sectors including the civil service, Africans were confined to the lowest rungs of manual, unskilled and semi-skilled positions. Workers in plantations, mines and construction were paid wages insufficient to feed and clothe themselves and their families at the minimal level. Their benefits were next to nothing. Semi-skilled European workers like drivers, where present, obtained ten times the pay of their African counterparts. They also garnered benefits like housing and health service. African workers in ports, industries, railways and civil service had to make do with pay levels one-tenth or less of that of the (exploited) workers engaged in similar occupations in Europe.

The small scale rural producers were in a worse situation. Their prime land was confiscated without compensation, and through force and harshly enforced taxation policies, they were made to grow crops like cotton, coffee, cashew nuts, sun flower and pyrethrum for export. They were paid a mere pittance, and relegated to perpetual back breaking, miserable existence.

Colonial powers utilized local elites, and foreign or indigenous traders, transporters, professionals and miscellaneous service providers to perform essential functions. These groups had a higher standard of living, better residential conditions and housing, and broader access to education and health care compared to the masses.

But the real beneficiaries were the foreign companies operating within or in connection with the colony, and the colonial power. The profit margins for the capital and consumer goods industries, trading conglomerates, banks, insurance houses, shipping companies and law firms having colonial operations were consistently high. Colonial operations also served as a protective buffer in times of minor or major economic crisis.

Rodney delivers a formidable case for the thesis that super exploitation of the colonized people and their resources generated super profits for the ruling nation. It was a system for large scale transfer of wealth (economic surplus) from Africa to Europe. He points out that European nations without African colonies and the USA also derived significant gains from the colonial system. The colonized people were a prime driver of Western development. And possession of colonies conferred economic, strategic and military advantage to the ruling power in relation to rival imperial nations. Colonized subjects also played crucial roles in its military campaigns.

## CHAPTER 6: COLONIALISM AS A SYSTEM FOR UNDERDEVELOPING AFRICA

Rodney then provides a comprehensive analysis of the other side of the issue covered in the last chapter: How did Africa benefit from colonialism? What were its short and long term consequences?

He first clarifies that he will not resort to a balance sheet oriented, bad versus good, approach to deal with the issue. Instead, he adopts a systemic framework. On consideration of the historic logic and political-economic forces that underlay colonial rule, he presents a detailed picture of life and trends affecting the different social groups in the colonized nations.

A typical colony is a three-tiered, top-down, grotesquely unequal society. At the top sit the Europeans who run governmental departments, or manage banks and other foreign firms. They live in segregated enclaves with all the manner of modern amenities. They are well remunerated and an inordinate amount of the state budget is directed for their safety and welfare. For example, in Ibadan, Nigeria in the 1940s, a well-equipped 11-bed hospital served some fifty Europeans while the half a million Africans were served by a 34-bed inferior health facility. And as the latter was likely utilized by the local elite, the masses basically had no public health facility at their disposal.

As noted earlier, the Europeans used local elements and/or external minorities to facilitate governance, economic policies, tax-collection, urban and rural commerce and provision of services. These intermediary groups often lived in reasonably maintained exclusive neighbourhoods with better housing, water, health and education services.

Over 95% of the colony's population, especially those in rural villages, lived in destitution with little or no services from the state. Colonialism was predicated on the logic of extraction of maximum amount of economic surplus for Europe. This implied remunerating and providing services to the producers of the wealth – the African peasants and workers – just to an extent that would keep the system in operation. And this policy was implemented with surgical precision. The facts and figures Rodney reveals in that regard are utterly shocking. Thus, after nearly five hundred years of rule, the Portuguese left Mozambique with only one doctor.

Beside exploding the myth of the alleged benevolent aspect of colonial rule, Rodney makes the crucial observation that the infrastructure, economic facilities, services and amenities put up during the colonial era, by design and in effect, entrenched the bonds of dependency on Europe. Roads, rail transport, ports and trade networks thereby served import/export activities. At the same time, internal and especially inter-regional trade was stifled.

The last two sections of this chapter are devoted to colonial education. It is shown that the education available for the indigenous population was both limited in extent and of inferior quality. Minuscule resources were devoted for a system geared to provide the lowest level literate cadres for the colony, and inculcate respect for and obedience towards the colonial rulers, their values, culture and history. Local knowledge and culture were branded inferior. An educated African was one who had discarded his traditions and adopted

European ways of dress, speech, behaviour and thought. The African was taught to despise his 'backward' fellow Africans.

Missionary schools focused on religion, rudimentary literacy and practical topics like agriculture, woodwork, basket making and brick laying. It was an implicit but rarely articulated tenet of the colonial ideology that for the most part, the African would not benefit from the standard, intellectually oriented education. Practical training, said to be suited for his mental calibre, would give him a means for earning a living.

Yet, Africans did not take this unfair situation lying down. Education was a prime arena for which local communities consistently petitioned the authorities for higher outlays, more teachers and expanded secondary schooling. Often, they built and ran their own schools. Even though colonial schooling was designed to instil a sense of loyalty to the rulers, some educated Africans threw off those mental shackles and assumed leadership positions in civic groups, trade unions, and agricultural cooperatives that went on to confront the discriminatory practices of the authorities, employers and traders. Eventually, not content with asking for crumbs within the colonial order, they were instrumental in the formation of political movements that struggled for full sovereignty.

This is what Rodney calls development by contradiction: an entity designed to serve the colonial system subsequently generated people who would dig its grave. Yet, he is aware of the limitations of the nationalist movements. The agenda of the educated elite differed in marked respects with the long-term interests of the peasants and workers. They were inclined to make compromises that facilitated the replacement of colonial rule with neo-colonial dependency. We got our own flag and national anthem, and the imperialists continued to reap immense benefits from our labour, land and resources.

## POSTSCRIPT

AM Babu writes on the sturdy foundation laid by Rodney to critique the development policies followed by post-colonial governments in Africa. Relying heavily on guidance, expertise and funding from global financial institutions and the imperial powers, these policies perpetuated, with minor modification, colonial economic structures. They generated some economic growth but not real development.

The local elite prospered but the conditions of the masses improved just a little. As the ability of Africa to stand on its own feet was stymied, its position relative to the West worsened. Much of the surplus generated in Africa continued to be siphoned off. Africa essentially remained an exporter of primary products and importer of manufactured goods, and that under unequal, exploitative terms of exchange.

Undue reliance on the world market and foreign investments is not a solution to Africa's woes. On the contrary, as Babu asserts, it is the primary *cause* of African underdevelopment. The continent can move in the direction genuine development that will generate sustained and substantial improvement in the lives of the broad masses by implementing policies that will progressively weaken the bonds of dependency on the imperial nations.

### A QUALIFICATION

My summary of each chapter of *HEUA* has focused on major points and historical approach. However, each chapter contains a wealth of examples that demonstrate the diversity of the historic process it covers. Taking these into consideration, we see that Rodney was not a formula driven analyzer of human society. He did not blindly adhere to the classical tenets of Marxism, dependency theory or Pan-Africanism. Though he was an unapologetic Marxist, his Marxism was cognizant of the terrain being covered. His notion of underdevelopment integrated internal-external economic structures with internal-external class relations. It depicted a complex system whose dynamics generated socio-ideological conditions that buttressed it as well as the forces that strove to transform it.

Though, Rodney wrote in a bold, uncompromising style, he did not resort to empty invective. His terminology was consistent, grounded in actuality and the finest principles of morality. In that regard he set a high standard for others seeking to integrate scholarship with humanistic activism.

### AN OVERALL VERDICT

Walter Rodney transformed in a major way how experts and ordinary people viewed Africa and its history. *HEUA* was a front-line promoter of the political-economy based framework for social analysis, influencing all types of Africa related societal studies. As a finely researched, integrated text glittering with pertinent examples and written in an eminently accessible style, it could not be ignored, even by the right wing. The major stimulus it provided for the application of a neglected scientific method to African societies effectively shifted the existing paradigm for conceptualizing African history. It divided modern African historiography into two distinct phases: pre- and post- *How Europe Underdeveloped Africa*.

The import of *HEUA* is captured by the galvanizing words of the endorsers of the 2011 edition. They tell us that its analytic approach is essential for understanding African history, and its key messages are directly relevant for the attainment of justice, equality and genuine development in the poor, dominated nations of the World to this day.

To quote four among them:

Rodney's classic study .... continues to provoke, educate and inspire – it resonates more than ever before. Angela Davis

A milestone in the history of Africa thinking for itself. Samir Amin

[A] legendary classic that has galvanized freedom fighters around the world. Cornel West

[It will] help in the development of updated strategies for challenging neo-liberal globalization and neo-colonialism. Bill Fletcher, Jr.

## QUESTIONS

With its publishing history and such praise from eminent personalities, what more needs to be said? Does not *HEUA* speak for itself? In the current era, the answer is both yes and no.

No, because *HEUA* is more than an academic work. It is also a potent weapon for challenging the *status quo*. As such it continues to be distorted and pilloried by the establishment. Academic bigwigs, development experts, politicians, political pundits and media persons by the majority say that while it may have had minor relevance when it came out, today it is of no value at all. They declare that socialism, the social system it promotes, is dead and buried for good. Moreover, Africans must stop blaming external forces for Africa's ills. The relevant question in their view is: How Africans are under-developing Africa?

And there are well-meaning Africanists who accept its historic significance, yet on the question of its present-day relevance, they concur with the right wing voices. Africa has changed so much that utilizing it to understand the current trends will do more harm than good, they solemnly proclaim. It is not anymore a useful guide for tackling modern Africa's litany of serious problems (Abdulazeez 2014; Mills 2011).

And there are left wing historians, few in number, who well appreciate the content and import of *HEUA*. They continue to assess Rodney's approach to history in academic conferences, books and technical papers published in peer reviewed journals. Their debates and opinions, generally cast in arcane academic formulations, are divided as well.

In the ideologically stultifying and trivialising climate of today, the detractors of *HEUA* are owed a comprehensive response. And even in the absence of such detractors, a need to confront critical queries about *HEUA* exists. In my view, this consideration applies to any work of major significance once decades or more have transpired since its inception. For *HEUA*, I pose three queries:

1. **Intrinsic quality:** Since 1972, an enormous amount of research on African history has been done. Developments of a methodological form have also occurred. In light of these, can we say that *HEUA* has stood the test of time, and retained its substantive and methodological value? Or has it essentially become dated?
2. **Practical value:** In the struggle for social change in Africa, does it continue to embody the import it had in the earlier days? Or have the conditions on the continent changed to such an extent that it cannot any longer either inspire activists or provide a useful guide to action?
3. **Pedagogic value:** Do today's students of African history, especially those in general undergraduate level classes, encounter either the type of material, or the Marxist framework for studying history, used in *HEUA*? If they do, what can we say about the way these items are presented?

To address these queries, the following pages examine the contents of *HEUA* and look at Rodney in his unitary persona as a historian, theoretician and activist. I identify and respond to the criticisms made to date of the content, style and practical value of *HEUA*, and then describe how modern day students encounter Rodney. For the latter task, a focused review of eight textbooks used in undergraduate level African history courses is conducted. These books span a wide range of approaches to history.

CHAPTER 2

## THE GLOBAL CONTEXT

From the end of World War II to roughly the mid-1970s, the capitalist-imperial order once more faced sustained challenges across the planet. As one after another of its hefty pillars shook, the era of self-determination, non-alignment and socialism bloomed. Victorious red revolutions in China, North Korea and North Vietnam, autonomy for India, Indonesia, Pakistan and the Philippines, and nationalistic coups in Egypt and the Middle East heralded the termination of direct colonial rule across Africa, Asia and the Caribbean. Socialist Cuba unveiled a novel, practical path of hope for humanity. Right in the belly of the beast, African Americans, Native Americans, Latinos, students, women's movements, workers and cultural activists embarked on humane itineraries marked with protests, occupations, boycotts and even armed resistance. Europe witnessed a tumultuous upswing of left-wing student, worker, cultural and feminist movements.

The imperialist powers responded with characteristic brutality and artful deviousness, at home and abroad. Patrice Lumumba, Malcolm X, Che Guevara and Oscar Romero (to name a few) were assassinated; ardent nationalists like Arbenz of Guatemala, Mossadegh of Iran, Allende of Chile and Nkrumah of Ghana were overthrown, a militarized massacre was instituted in Indonesia, and CIA-backed death squad regimes mushroomed – these were but some of their atrocious deeds. Such setbacks notwithstanding, on the whole, the march of ordinary folk across the planet for genuine justice and liberation grew in strength. The success of the Cuban revolution in 1959, the forced departure of France from Algeria, the ousting of the US from Vietnam in 1974, the ejection of Portugal from its colonies in Africa, the extirpation of the US-backed dictator of Nicaragua by the Sandinista and majority rule for Zimbabwe constituted some of the shining milestones of this righteous journey.

## MENTAL LIBERATION

Struggle in the street went hand in hand with endeavours to liberate the mind. Rigid modes of thought underpinning and rationalizing the *status quo* faced vibrant challenges in the media, literature and academia. From law and psychology to art, from sociology and economics to health, no discipline evaded critical inquiry. The 1960s saw a creative, expansive flowering of ideas in these fields. New avenues of mass and scholarly communication materialized. The visions of stellar radical thinkers of earlier eras not only gained renewed appeal but were also examined anew and qualitatively expanded. And it was a worldwide phenomenon.

Under the pioneering works of Frantz Fanon and CLR James, activist thinkers of Africa like Samir Amin, Dennis Brutus, Amilcar Cabral, Ruth First, Archie Mafeje, Bernard Magubane, Albert Memmi, Félix Moumié, Kwame Nkrumah, and Julius Nyerere crafted keen expositions analysing why the world was as it was, and charted potential directions for change. Elsewhere, in a similar vein, Ernesto Che Guevara, Josue De Castro, Oliver C Cox, Eduardo Galeano, Paulo Freire and Eric Williams (Latin America and the Caribbean); Paul Baran, Noam Chomsky, Angela Davis, Michael Harrington, William Hinton, George L Jackson, Martin Luther King, Gabriel Kolko, James Petras, Paul Sweezy, Malcolm X and Howard Zinn (North America); Simone de Beauvoir, Charles Bettleheim, Aimé Césaire, Regis Debray, André Gunder Frank, Erich Fromm, Eric Hobsbawm, RD Laing, Oscar Lange, Ernest Mandel, Herbert Marcuse, Jean-Paul Sartre and Bertrand Russell (Europe and the UK); and Eqbal Ahmad, Tariq Ali, Waldon Bello, Ho Chin Minh, DD Kosambi, EMS Namboodiripad and Edward Said (Asia and the Middle East) formulated new vistas in humanistic and scientific ideas that germinated from an internationalist ethic, consistent logic, and sound factual foundations. Walter Rodney, with multinational roots in Guyana, the Caribbean and Africa, was a shining light in this stellar group.

Cultural arenas like music, songs, poetry, film, theatre, literature and fine art flowered along directions distinctly discordant with the Hollywood led escapist panorama. To name but a few of the literary stars of that era: Ayi Kwei Armah, James Baldwin, Nawal El-Saadawi, Nadime Gordimer, Nazim Hikmet, Ibrahim Hussein, Yashar Kamel, Alex LaGuma, Gabriel Garcia Marquez, Sembene Ousmane, José Saramago, Wole Soyinka, Ngũgĩ wa Thiong'o and Pramoedya Ananta Toer entertained, enlightened and emboldened large intercontinental audiences with hopes dreams even as their surroundings retained much of the ugliness of the bygone days.

Within the discipline of history in particular, specific investigations under an interdisciplinary, socio-economic approach took greater hold. Micro-studies morphed into impressive regional and global narratives. Of the works in this genre, I have in mind JD Bernal's four volume *Science and Society* (1954), DD Kosambi's *An Introduction to the Study of Indian History* (1956), Gordon Childe's *What Happened in History* (1960), Basil Davidson's *Africa: History of a Continent* (1966), AG Frank's *Capitalism and Underdevelopment in Latin America* (1967), Eduardo Galeano's *Open Veins of Latin America* (1974), Samir Amin's *Accumulation on a World Scale* (1978) and Howard Zinn's *A People's History of the United States* (1980).

Walter Rodney's *HEUA* was an integral member of this lofty collection. An erudite, novel work of African history, it effectively critiqued the camouflaged liberal or explicitly pro-imperial narratives prevalent till then. It thoroughly countered the conservative slant on African history in the widely-used books like *A Short History of Africa* by Oliver and Fage. As a readable text, Rodney's book was hailed by Pan-Africanists, progressive scholars, students, activists and freedom fighters. Though, for the local and Western reactionaries, in academia and outside, it was an object of spiteful vitriol. Its Marxist methodology, forthright style and uncompromising verdict engendered a sharp binary divide among social scientists and historians, including of the left. As noted earlier, it came to be *the line* for demarcating modern African historiography into two main periods.

Within a few years, it was a required or reference text for courses in African History, World History and African Studies at the undergraduate and graduate levels in Africa, Asia, the Caribbean, Europe and North America. In Tanzania, it entered the high school history curriculum as well. Students, scholars and regular readers now obtained a more authentic version of the past of a regularly misrepresented continent. Directly and indirectly, it spawned a large body of research and writing in history and other social sciences that utilized a pan-Africanist, anti-imperial, Marxist orientation. Manning Marable's *How Capitalism Underdeveloped Black America: Problems in Race, Political Economy, and Society*, to take one case, does not just reflect its influence in the title but more so in the conceptual framework utilized.

A rounded explication of the mammoth, complex blooming of the intellect of the 1960s requires a book by itself. But, what I have covered provides a fair idea of its scope. Those extensions of mental, moral and political horizons guided the youth and social movements in all lands towards progressive, anti-imperial activism, which in turn fertilized the world of radical ideas. In Africa and the Caribbean, this ferment signified the beginnings of mental decolonization of the post-colonial generation. No longer at ease with the appalling economic reality and hollow rhetoric of flag independence, they internalized the radical conceptions and began to stir.

By 1971, schools and colleges across Africa were in a state of turmoil. Hardly had the dust from the anti-colonial struggles settled, the seekers of a genuinely brighter future began to confront neo-colonialism as well as their conniving, inept, authoritarian local rulers. *HEUA* entered the scene at right time to further educate and propel the restless youth and progressive leaders of Africa, the Caribbean and elsewhere towards an effective philosophy and strategy to confront imperialist domination and the internal subjugation of the masses.

As the Chinese youth held up the quotations of Chairman Mao, the progressive African and Caribbean youth thumbed through Fanon's *The Wretched of the Earth*, Nkrumah's *Neo-Colonialism: The Highest Stage of Imperialism*, and Rodney's *How Europe Underdeveloped Africa* for knowledge, inspiration and guidance.

## Chapter 3

## A GRAND REVERSAL

But these valiant struggles suffered major setbacks. Four decades on, the global reality has altered fundamentally. The socialist camp is no more. Unbridled capitalism has re-established its hegemony in every nook and cranny of the planet. From Washington to Moscow, from Paris to Peking, markets, liberalization, privatization and investors run the show. The land of Mao is a capitalist power house while the US/NATO military forces spread mayhem where they please. Even Cuba has partially yielded, and faces mighty pressure to re-join the neo-liberal fold.

In Africa, neo-colonial domination is solidly entrenched. Most of the earlier attempts at economic self-determination such as the local import substitution industries that sprang up after Independence, qualitatively limited as they were, have been decimated under the fierce onslaught of the World Bank/IMF led policies. Africa is locked under the tutelage of global capital as Western, Chinese and other giant corporations plunder its land, labour and resources with the firm assistance of the local bourgeoisie and corrupt political elite (Burgis 2015). (For scores of well documented, revealing examples from across the continent, explore the websites www.africafocus.org and www.pambazuka.org).

Despite that ugly reality, popular consciousness does not view the West as the economically exploitative entity it truly is but, instead, it has been reborn as the fountain of freedom, democracy, humanitarian assistance, social development and modern culture. It is now seen as a generous funder of health, education health and social services, and supporter of free and fair elections, good governance and much more.

We regularly witness acts and pronouncements that make a mockery of even the nominal independence of African nations. The litany of unilateral Western military interventions in recent years have lacked any semblance of accountability and violated the basic norms of international law. These powers also interfere in local African affairs brazenly in major and minor social, political and cultural arenas daily (Turse 2015).

Such a drastic reversal in the African economic and political reality has accompanied an equally dismal reversal in the arenas of culture, ideas and outlook. The progressive visions from the past have largely been expunged from memory and scholarly discourse. History has bitten the dust as the intellectual and practical efforts of that era for a world based on equality and universal dignity are a mystery to the modern African youth. Little from the massive intellectual edifice developed in that era garners even a passing attention in the academia and mass media today. And when it does, it is in derogatory or dismissive tones. The grotesque violations of human rights perpetrated in the name of socialism (like those in Cambodia under Pol Pot) are repeated while the equally horrific or worse crimes of capitalism (like the murderous US aggressions in Indochina, Central America and Iraq) are swept under the rug.

The dominant tone is: "those misguided leftist ideas only compounded Africa's social and economic problems; the modern world has no room for the totalitarianism they espoused; democracy, individual initiative, private investment and free trade promise the best future for humanity, including Africa."

## THE RESILIENT ONES

It is not that the entire intellectual edifice of that era has been reduced to ashes. That cannot be. With its unique mix of veracity, logic and ethics, with its appeal to the sense of justice, a socialist vision is by now integral to human thought. Activists and committed scholars, old and new, will invariably keep the flame alight. But currently, it is a vision with but a tiny audience. The cacophonous dominant media drown out the voices that even faintly appear to support it. As they lose broad appeal, socialists and anti-imperialists converse, utilizing arcane and elusive terminology, among themselves. Dejected, many adopt a stance that does not query the capitalist-imperial system as such. While noting its multitude of major problems, they pursue reformist, specific, NGO-based goals within that allegedly unquestionable system.

Nevertheless, a few elements of anti-capitalistic thought have withstood the gale force winds of bourgeois ideology. A few have even broadened their reach. Creative gems from Ngũgĩ and Saramago still command a good audience. Zinn's opus has a stable following in the USA and has spawned an impressive line of derivative works including Vijay Prashad's *The Darker Nations: A People's History of the Third World* and R Dunbar-Ortiz's *An Indigenous Peoples' History of the United States*.

But in general, the thinkers of that era, including the towering figures like Amin, Cabral, Chomsky, Sembene and Said retain but a tiny readership. Che is a commercialized, romantic icon; the modern youth who flaunt his badges have no clue as to what he stood for. Martin Luther King Day, a holiday in the USA, is a day for the expression of unbridled consumerism that is decorated with a one-sided presentation of his real legacy.

Among the progressive intellectual fare from that era that still command a decent audience, one resilient baobab stands out: Rodney's epic *How Europe Underdeveloped Africa*.

In print continuously since 1972, it has secured a better global presence in the education system and general readership than most of the premier progressive books from those days. It is still the subject of occasional conferences and seminars in universities in Africa, Europe and America (see Wikipedia (2014) for a partial list). And, it still attracts hostile diatribe from right wing elements. Not content with assassinating the man, they seek to bury his ideas too. But this giant of a human being continues to haunt them from his grave.

What accounts for the global impact and sustained popularity of a book written in Tanzania forty and some years ago and brought out by two small publishing houses? Before answering this question, a few words on Rodney, the man, and the brand of historiography embedded in his book are in order.

CHAPTER 4

# RODNEY THE REVOLUTIONARY

Walter Rodney (1942-1980) was not just a brilliant radical historian but as well, a public intellectual *par excellence*, a revolutionary firmly devoted to the cause of human emancipation from injustice and exploitation in all their varied forms. His grassroots level involvement in societal ferments, no matter where he was, attested to his unwavering internationalism and commitment. Neo-colonial regimes, conservative scholars and the embassies of Western nations denounced him. Yet his genuinely warm spirit, exquisite oratory skills, extroverted personality, critical articles in the mass media and participation in the day-to-day struggles cemented his popularity with students, Pan-Africanists and anti-imperialist activists, and ordinary people in Africa, the Caribbean, Guyana and elsewhere.

After completing his doctoral studies, apart from a tumultuous year at the University of West Indies and eight months in Cuba, he lectured at the History Department of the University of Dar es Salaam until 1974. During that period, he was the most popular lecturer and progressive persona on the campus. His in-depth command of history, ability to logically critique the conventional historical narratives and articulate his case in a clear style combined with an operatically melodious tone made his lectures a once-in-a-lifetime experience for the students.

The University of Dar es Salaam was by then the prime center for the flowering of progressive ideas in Africa. Inspired by Mwalimu Nyerere's sustained commitment to African liberation and the announced policy of socialism and self-reliance, scholars of high esteem in a wide range of disciplines from other African nations and abroad visited the campus for short and long time periods. A vibrant part of the student body and local scholars were involved in national and pan-African activism, progressive reform in the organization of education and developing a curriculum that reflected the values of and requirements for building a socialist society. The University Students' African Revolutionary Front (USARF), comprised of leftist students from Tanzania and neighboring African nations, led the student activism on the campus and beyond.

It was an ideal atmosphere for the scholar-activist Rodney. He engaged closely with the academic, student-based, national and African liberation oriented struggles, both at the practical and theoretical level. His actions included staying in *Ujamaa* (cooperative) villages, giving talks in schools, debating other academics in the public arena, and writing newspaper columns, popular works and scholarly papers. Despite many a hostile brush offs with the powers that be, he went on with his activism and radical writings. (Further details on Rodney's work at the University of Dar es Salaam are given in Chapter 9.)

He left Dar es Salaam in 1974 to assume the position of Professor of History at the University of Guyana, the land of his birth. But that did not last, as the neo-colonial rulers soon had him ejected from academia. This did not lead to abatement of his activism. He co-founded and became a part of the collective leadership of the Working Peoples Alliance, whose aim was to fight for a just, non-racial, socialistic society. Just as the Alliance was making major headways, Rodney's life was tragically cut down by a car bomb, decidedly of imperialist/state origin, on 13 June 1980. The involvement of the Guyanese government of Forbes Burnham in his murder, which was stated in the Introduction of the 1981 edition of *HEUA*, has now been confirmed officially. The Walter Rodney Commission of Inquiry, in its 2016 report to the Guyanese authorities, noted that there was sufficient evidence to show that the armed forces and state security organs were behind the assassination, and subsequent cover up and deflection of blame (see www.walterrodneyfoundation.org for further information).

This is but a brief sketch of Rodney's activism and its ramifications. For a fuller portrayal, see the Introduction to the 1981 edition by Harding, Strickland and Hill, and biographical works such as Alpers and Fontaine (1982;1985), Campbell (1985), Chung (2013), Creighton (2000), Drake and Lalljie (2009), Gabriehu (2003), Hirji (2013), Kwayana (2013), Lewis (1998), Othman (2005), Salky (1974), Shivji (1993;2012), Swai (1981;1982), Wamba dia Wamba (1980) and Wikipedia (2014).

Suffice it to say that Walter Rodney was a humane revolutionary and radical scholar in the finest and fullest sense of these terms. He strove bravely and tirelessly to change society in words and deeds. In that regard, he stands shoulder to shoulder in the reified company of Norman Bethune, Amilcar Cabral, Frantz Fanon, Ernesto Che Guevara, Chris Hani, ML King, Rosa Luxemburg, Ho Chi Minh, PG Pinto, Paul Robeson, MN Roy, Leon Trotsky, Malcolm X and many others.

Walter Rodney remains in our memories for the same reasons that these exceptional human beings remain in our memories: for dedicating and sacrificing their lives to uplifting humanity from the yolk of capitalist and imperialist tyranny and to endeavor to construct a just, humane society on this planet.

## Chapter 5

## RODNEY AND HISTORIOGRAPHY

The standard works on African history produced during the colonial era fell along two main strands. The pro-imperial, plainly racist, strand depicted Africa prior to the arrival of the Europeans as a bleak continent populated by uncivilized tribes engaged in primitive modes of living and continual local conflict. It was claimed that Africa, particularly the sub-Saharan areas, had had no machinery of the state to speak of. Hence the outsiders were doing its people a favor by imposing a sense of order, civility and material progress onto their lives.

The other, the liberal, Africanist strand, conceded that Africa had, on its own, made some strides towards a civilized way of life. But the continent now needed assistance from Europe to become a modernized place. It also conceded that the colonial powers had not always behaved in a just or decent manner towards the people of African. But the past was the past. A partnership based on harmony and mutual interests of both the parties was now advisable and essential for Africa to progress.

Both strands reflected the visions and interests of the respective colonial powers as they both accepted that colonial rule had to continue, at least for the foreseeable future. As the struggles for independence matured across Africa, these versions of its history faced mounting criticisms. Sympathetic scholars not only brought out more accurate versions of African history prior to the arrival of the white man but the oppressive and unjust facets of colonialism were more fully detailed as well.

The anti-colonial African historiography itself had two main strands. One, the Afrocentric strand, focused on highlighting the situation in Africa prior to the landing of the Europeans. The glorious empires and kingdoms of the past were emphasized and projected as the basis for a return to true African values and practices. The lesson from that strand was that the future for Africa lay in the resumption of its long interrupted trajectory of autonomous evolution on the social, political and cultural fronts.

The nation-building strand also highlighted the injustices of colonial rule. But it did not advocate a total break with this era. Claiming that colonial rule had generated some beneficial outcomes for the indigenous people, principally in education, health, the system of justice, transport, and the economy, it advocated that African nations should not discard such gains. Instead, they should extend them to wider segments of their populations. Reforming the laws and practices that had earlier restricted the benefits to a minority was on the agenda. In this task, Europe would partner with Africa to help it develop the economy, modernize social institutions and democratize the governance structures.

As more and more African nations attained political independence, it was the nation-building strand that dominated the historical and political circles.

The picture painted of the past by the Afrocentric and the nation-building historians was circumscribed by their orientation and premises. A key sector minimally touched in their discourses was the economy. And when it was, it was done in ways that presented a partial picture of the reality. Not that these two strands of histories were monolithic. Within each, a range of views, some more progressive than others, were present.

In the meantime, a third strand had been evolving in the background. Barely visible in the colonial era, it gathered steam particularly after the mid-1960s. By then it had become apparent that the pledges by Europe and the US of mutually beneficial partnerships with Africa were distinctively false and abundantly hypocritical. Political independence did not imply economic autonomy or progress. The global powers continued to dominate Africa in trade, investment and finance. They basically decided the what, how and when of African economic activities. As in the past, these economies would primarily serve the demands of external economies. Internal benefits would be restricted mostly to the elite strata but the vast majority of the inhabitants would continue to endure grinding poverty and misery.

This socio-political disjunction between high expectations and decidedly limited outcomes for the masses provided a fertile ground for the political economy based Marxist strand of African history to thrive. By according primary attention to economic factors, it demonstrated with a mountain of facts and figures that since the initial contact, Europe had conducted itself in single-minded, exceedingly exploitative ways towards Africa. Since the economic structures established during the colonial days changed but to a minor extent after Independence, development on the economic and social fronts was also constrained and unequal. Marxist and socialist economists and historians like Samir Amin, CLR James, Eric Williams and Jack Woddis unearthed volumes of evidence showing how diverse mechanisms of such exploitative linkages operated in different nations and at different times. This new scholarship was not restricted to history but was an integral aspect of the radicalization of social sciences and general thought in the 1960s.

Walter Rodney's framework for conceptualizing history derived from the tenets of Marxist political economy. He began with the monumental foundation laid by Karl Marx and Fredreich Engels that was subsequently extended to cover the phase of monopoly capitalism and imperialism by VI Lenin. On top of that, he was influenced, to one degree or another, by left leaning theorists like Samir Amin, Paul Baran, Oliver Cox, Frantz Fanon, AG Frank, P Jalee, CLR James, Kwame Nkrumah, Julius Nyerere and T Szentes. Yet, he was no mechanical borrower of ideas. Always a critical scholar, his theoretical framework evolved over time as he engaged in ideological and practical struggles with comrades and adversaries.

Rodney's theoretical framework matured towards a unique blend of classical Marxism, modern conceptualization of theories of imperialism and principled Pan-Africanism. In my summaries of the chapters of *HEUA*, I provided an introduction to Rodney's conceptual framework. Now, cognizant of the possibility of oversimplification once again, I am drawn to list, in an abbreviated form, the ten primary tenets that underscored his framework for historical analysis:

1. Human labor (physical and mental, skilled and unskilled) is the sole source of value (wealth) in human society. What the economists call capital is but congealed or accumulated labor. Hence, to say that money makes more money, or that taxpayers and donors fund the development budget is to utter a surface level half-truth. Ultimately, all revenue streams in society arise from the expenditure, somewhere, of human labor.
2. Human society functions in a dynamically integrated manner. While a degree of specialized scrutiny is essential for understanding this process, it is ultimately inadequate and misleading to view society purely in terms of autonomous segments like the economy, politics, culture, history, race, gender, ethnicity, and so on.
3. Human society is perpetually in a state of flux. Societal change, gradual (quantitative) or transformative (qualitative), is not a uniformly or similarly paced process everywhere. Uneven development and variation are the norm.
4. Social class, defined in terms of ownership and/or control of

wealth, the means of generating it, and the avenues for appropriating it, is the primary unit of analysis for understanding how modern human societies function. The tensions and cohesiveness between social classes paradoxically constitute both the primary factors for stability as well as the basic drivers of long term change.
5. Social change is a dialectical process. Frequently, aspects of the superstructure (a collective term for societal sectors like politics, state institutions, law, culture, education and the media) decisively affect the nature, direction and duration of the transformation experienced by human society.
6. Over the past two millennia, sub-Saharan African societies became increasingly divided into social classes.
7. Over the past five centuries, the capitalist system that evolved in the West became a unified global system with two main interrelated parts: the dominant (developed, industrialized, wealthy, imperialist) nations and the dominated (underdeveloped, primary production based, poor, subjugated) nations.
8. Since the European contacts of the 15th century, African societies have increasingly operated under the rubric of the capitalist system. But external powers ensured that the features of capitalism they acquired restricted them to be dependent, exploited entities within that system. Colonial policies, rules and actions were, on an on-going basis, designed to prevent the emergence of mature and autonomous capitalist economies in Africa.
9. Class relations in Africa in the present era are internal (national) and external (transnational) in scope. Failure to take either component adequately into account produces a flawed picture of the African socio-economic-political-cultural reality, past or present.
10. Genuine development for African nations requires the masses take control of state power, begin to disengage from the global capitalist system, adopt socialism and use the economic surplus they produce for their own benefit.

Rodney's approach posits capitalism as a global system that transcends national boundaries. The system is propelled by conflicts and cohesiveness between the economic classes within and across these boundaries. Imperialism is primarily an economic phenomenon but it also has sturdy political, military, and cultural pillars. It encompasses direct (colonial) and indirect (neo-colonial) domination. Intricate and pervasive structures of dependency are the prime mechanisms that facilitate the extraction of economic surplus from the dominated nations to the dominant ones, from the subjugated classes to the ruling classes.

Imperial rule generates underdevelopment. That, however, does not mean that no expansion of economic activities occurs. To the contrary, a new railway line may be built; the output of cotton, sisal and gold may expand rapidly; and the value of exports and imports may increase too. These economic activities are initially stimulated by imposing unfair taxes on the local population to force them to seek employment or grow export crops. The coercive measures are relaxed as the entrenchment of dependency makes the process self-perpetuating. The wages of the plantation workers or the buying price for cotton from the farmers condemn their families to a life of poverty and ill health. The local economy serves external economies and the benefits accrue mostly imperial companies and external capitalists. The evolution of such structural dependence goes hand in hand with the establishment of political, social and cultural institutions that reinforce and complement it.

Rodney thus demarcates the idea of economic growth from economic development. Though the long-term task is primarily an economic one, he acknowledges that socio-political factors will play a critical role in initiating and propelling the struggle in the transition period. His framework for viewing the past logically paved the way for a critique of the World Bank inspired post-colonial policies that mainly promoted expansion of the very types of economic activities established in the colonial era. The 'aid' and loans from outside constitute but a small portion of the wealth extracted from Africa by the imperial entities. Rodney's analysis implies that the strategy of internally-oriented, integrated economic development is the sole avenue for emancipation of African nations. The Postscript by AM Babu succinctly lays down the main elements of such a strategy, and complements the main text.

For a decent introduction to Marxist thought, see D'Amato (2006).

## Chapter 6

## CRITICISMS OF THE BOOK

The popularity and anti-imperial stance of *HEUA* made it a target of unsparing criticism from elitist, right wing quarters. And its method, contents and conclusions as well underwent sharp scrutiny from some progressive academics.

The key flaws of *HEUA* were said to be: (i) It converts history into a rigid deterministic process; (ii) it reduces human existence to the material dimension; (iii) it accords the principal, if not the sole, weight to external factors; (iv) it denies agency to the African people; (v) its terminology is too polemical; (vi) it is more like a political propaganda tract than a scholarly work; (vii) it is not a Marxist work because it side lines class relations; (viii) it is an expression of racially biased black nationalism; (ix) it does not depict the role of women in African history; and (x) it is factually inaccurate on many counts. Several of these points are interrelated.

Below I examine these criticisms in a point by point manner.

### RIGIDITY

The claim that *HEUA* employs a rigid approach for elucidating history is not unique. Regularly levied onto works that derive from the Marxist method, it has its roots in a misperceived aspect of that method. Unlike for the varied branches of bourgeois social science, the fundamental tenets of Marxism are clearly identifiable. Because of that, Marxist historians are accused of applying these tenets reflexively, thus promoting a formula driven method of conceptualizing human society. The fact that many Soviet era books were written in a standardized way lends a degree of credibility to this charge.

To assess this claim, I resort to an analogy from biology. Ward and Kirschvink (2015) pose the question: What is life? One definition they put forward is that a living entity (i) metabolizes, (ii) has complexity and organization, (iii) reproduces, (iv) develops, (v) evolves, and (vi) is autonomous. Another more succinct definition of life they give is: 'Life is a chemical system capable of Darwinian evolution' (pp 32—35). Both definitions posit a few simple tenets. Yet, each forms a foundation on the basis of which we can capture and explain a complex biosphere comprising of millions of distinctive life processes and organisms. Those myriad of beautiful forms of nature are depicted in a systematic fashion in biology books. The message is: a simple, terse functional foundation can be consistent with a majestically varied edifice. A scientific approach to explicate an elaborate natural or social reality can be based on the tenets of such a foundation. To discover these tenets is a primary aim of science. The relevant queries are: Do they form a logical and coherent system? Are they empirically valid? Is the theoretical system based on them aligned with the trends in the natural or social domain?

Compared to the natural sciences, application of the scientific method to history has many limitations. They stem from the inaccurate, restricted and biased nature of the information available. But it does not mean that we should not apply conceptual rigor and the scientific method to history. In this discipline as well, identification of basic laws (tenets) of societal stability and change is a key task. Applying them critically to information from historical research, one can write scientific works that sparkle with creativity. Deficiencies in the raw material at hand and the complexity of the phenomenon are not a license to, as post-modernists are inclined to do, fly off on speculative, empirically dubious tangents.

Elements of creative interpretability are evident in classic Marxist works like Engels' *The Rise of the Family, Private Property and the State* and VI Lenin's *The Development of Capitalism in Russia*. The voluminous outputs of later Marxists like Samir Amin, JD Bernal, Gordon Childe, AG Frank, Eduardo Galeano, Eric Hobsbawm, CLR James, DD Kosambi, Paul Sweezy and Howard Zinn as well display extensive methodological and interpretive novelty and creativity. Their well-researched works interweave multiple facets of human society into elaborate but logical tapestries. Walter Rodney, as any decent venture into *HEUA* reveals, belongs to this group of Marxist writers who did not have a formula driven approach to the study of human society. His earlier book, *History of the Upper Guinea Coast, 1540 to 1800*, persuasively enjoins a wide range of information to construct a narrative brimming with insightful, glittering gems.

Sterile scholarship affects all brands of history, Marxist and non-Marxist. To declare that Marxist renditions of history are, by default, formula driven signifies either lack of familiarity with this creative arena of intellectual activity, or a politically motivated diatribe, or what is most likely, both. I continue to elaborate this point below.

## FACTS AND THEORY

Any endeavor in the natural or social science faces the chicken-or-egg dilemma: Commence with a theory and gather facts, or collect facts, then formulate the theory.

Most scientists declare preference for an empiricist stand on this issue: Facts first, theory next. Sherlock Holmes, Arthur Conan Doyle's master sleuth, prescribed an identical tenet:

> It is a capital mistake to theorize before one has data. Insensibly one begins to twist facts to suit theories, instead of theories to suit facts.

Since *HEUA* begins with a well-defined framework for historic analysis, it is said to be fitting facts to a preconceived, one-fits-all version of history. That accusation, like that of rigidity, is invalid. First, as noted above, a terse conceptual foundation does not necessarily make the output a fixed and dry one. Second, the facts-first view overlooks the reality that science does not emerge from a series of separate, unique events. It is not a conglomeration of discrete facts, snapshots or events about nature, society or persons. Science develops as a cumulative process, building on the work of other scientists, past and present. At each stage, an *a priori* theory exists. The new work may confirm, alter, augment or negate it. Many theories emerge along the way. Far from being a haphazard collection of information, science research is a systematic process guided by a preliminary understanding of the phenomenon under study. That knowledge affects the kind and volume of facts that are deemed relevant, and the design of the scheme for acquiring them.

For example, an epidemiological investigation of whether an industrial chemical increases the risk of lung cancer must account for age and smoking status, the known risk factors for the disease. The researcher begins with a theory that involves these two factors. They should be incorporated into the design of the new study, type and manner of data collection, and the analysis of the collected data.

Facts and theory follow a Hegelian dialectic. Theory guides the research process but the new data may change it, at times markedly. To separate the two aspects of science in an abstract manner is not reflective of the actuality of science.

Despite its empiric limitations, research in history follows that scheme. Consciously or not, historians proceed on the basis of some vision of the historic reality. How they perceive social change is influenced by one or another model for understanding society. That model affects the kind of research conducted, the methods of data collection, the type of data collected, and as important, the kind of data not collected. Processing and organizing the collected data, and the eventual write up is also guided by those historiographical predilections.

The Marxist and other historians differ in a principal aspect. For the former, the guiding theoretical framework is laid out clearly and openly. The *status quo* inclined historians, operating under an illusory claim of objectivity, utilize background tenets that are usually not explicitly stated. And when they are, they are presented in an elusive, diffuse, distorted or incomplete manner.

Take John Illife's *Africans: The History of a Continent* (Iliffe 2007). In this well-regarded text, he opines that the continent's 'unique population history' makes 'demographic growth' the basic principle for deciphering its distant and recent past. He goes further: 'The modern histories of all Third World nations need to be rewritten around demographic growth' (p 2). That is an unambiguous declaration of a theoretical framework: that population growth is the principal factor driving social and economic advancement. Even as its empirical and conceptual validity is open to question, and his application to African history hardly establishes its veracity, that declaration does not generate controversy. It does not elicit the charge of rigidity or putting theory before data. Why not? Because not only do many mainstream historians ascribe to that tenet but also, its application does not entail unmasking the mechanisms of the capitalist, imperialist system. Instead, it elicits the standard recipe given to Africa by Western think tanks and funders: Curb population growth and you will prosper.

Another case: MK Asante in *The History of Africa* (Asante 2007) decries the lack of 'thematic centrality' in African history. To cover that deficiency, his book utilizes the Afrocentric framework. Regarded as a leading work in that genre, the key tenets of its theory are, however, not defined with any degree of clarity.

Again, we have a paradox: On the one hand, historians lament the lack of an organizing framework. But when one is given, and especially if it is of the political economy variety, its merit is set aside. It is by definition dismissed as deterministic. The contrasting treatments accorded to Rodney, on one side, and Illife and Asante, on the other, reflect a standard practice. In history, as in the other social sciences, the Marxist approach is regularly judged according to harsher, more elusive standards. If, following Rodney, you were to declare that the modern history of Africa should be rewritten around the evolution of structures of dependency, it would instantly raise loud alarm bells in the profession: How can you prejudge history? You would be prejudged.

Even a cursory examination of the evidence you have marshalled would not be done. 'It simply cannot be true,' the distinguished professors from the renowned ivory towers of the West would reflexively proclaim.

Those who charge Marxist writing with rigidity blithely ignore the numerous creative, flexible works produced by Marxist historians from all the corners of the globe. In relation to Africa, the reference and reading list in Freund (1998) gives a good picture of the vast scope of such creative scholarly output.

The Indian historian DD Kosambi, who exercised a significant influence on a generation of students of Indian history, is a specific case in point. In his pioneering 1956 book, *An Introduction to the Study of Indian History*, he identifies his historiographical scheme by defining history as 'the presentation, in chronological order, of successive developments in the means and relations of production' (Kosambi 1956, p 1). That classic Marxist stand notwithstanding, what he subsequently does is to roundly critique Karl Marx. He calls the notion of the Asiatic mode of production, used by Marx to explicate Asian societies, seriously flawed. Nonetheless, he also asserts that the political-economy approach developed by Marx remains an eminently useful, scientific method for the study of human society. Applying that method in an innovative, multidisciplinary fashion to India, he gives us a novel, consistent, fascinating picture of the trajectory of early India. One important arena pioneered by Kosambi was the analysis of the coinage of the day to cast light on social and economic features of the social order (see Guha 2013; Kosambi 2013; Thapar 2013). Howard Zinn, who corrected the intense patriotic, elitist bias found in the standard US history texts and approached that history from the conditions and viewpoints of ordinary people, is another mesmerizingly creative Marxist historian (Zinn 1980).

*HEUA* is cast in the same light. Even as it employs Marx's insights into how human history unfolds, it does not blindly apply the modes of production scheme Marx proposed for Europe to Africa. Though it utilizes key concepts formulated by Marxists like VI Lenin, P Baran and AG Frank to explain the African reality under imperialism, it does not do that in a routine manner.

Importantly, *HEUA* does not succumb to the strictly structural variety of the development of underdevelopment model. It attends to the internal class structures and is cognizant of the importance, dominant at times, of the superstructure in historic change. Rodney's explanation of why, unlike Europe, China did not autonomously evolve into a developed capitalist society is one example. His analysis of the contradictory impact of colonial education in Africa shows the scientifically adaptable nature of his methodology. Overall, his book does not mimic a scheme adopted from a standard text. On the contrary, it uses available historic evidence to indicate which of the social, political or economic factors and actors played critical roles at specific geographic locations and points in time. Further, these disparate factors are connected within an overall systemic framework.

## PRIMACY OF ECONOMICS

True to his Marxist stance, Rodney declares economic factors as the primary drivers of African history. He thereby is deemed guilty of not just the sin of determinism but worse, of economic determinism.

Firstly, note the fact that today most historians dealing with Africa give noticeable weight to economic factors, at least into the presentation of the situation up to the end of colonial rule. Only a rare chronicler of the past disputes the primacy of the economic motives for colonialism. Yet, what is rarely acknowledged is that this historiographical transformation in no small measure reflects the long-term influence of the Marxist historians active in the sixties, among whom Rodney was the leading light.

Second, double standards extend to this issue as well. Establishment historians are not immune from succumbing to biologic, genetic, or race based deterministic explanations. Yet, we do not hear Asante (2007) being taken to task for narrow cultural determinism or Ilife (2007) being castigated for simplistic demographic determinism. Why then does economic determinism, real or alleged, cause a widespread uproar?

Rodney's critique of the bulk of the historians of Africa was that they not only ignored or marginalized the essential economic issues but also that when they considered the racial, tribal, religious, cultural, behavioral or environmental factors, they did so in a disjointed manner. They either failed to utilize or, at best, presented in a masked fashion, known facts about the exceedingly exploitative dimensions of the African economic reality. Hence, their narrowly framed histories served more to justify slavery, colonial domination and neo-colonialism than to enlighten us about the African past and present. They as well favored post-colonial trajectories for Africa that were essentially pro-imperial in substance.

Interestingly, it may be noted that a few heavy weight right wing analysts of societal change have advocated their own quite rigid yet empirically hollow forms of economic determinism (Rostow 1960). And these have served to rationalize past and recent Western economic inroads into the dominated nations.

Rodney's strident expose of their pro-*status quo* bias decidedly unnerved the mainstream historians. And they responded with the usual diversionary tactics. Charges of inflexible economic determinism automatically arose. Dismissals of Marxist analysis of society along these lines hark back to ancient days. But such a charge was effectively rebuffed by Engels a long way back.

> According to the materialist conception of history, the ultimately determining element in history is the production and reproduction of real life. Other than this neither Marx nor I have ever asserted. Hence if somebody twists this into saying that the economic element is the only determining one, he transforms that proposition into a meaningless, abstract, senseless phrase (Engels 1890).

A foundational aspect of Rodney's economic thinking generally escapes attention. As noted earlier, following Marx, he held that human labour – routine or creative, unskilled or skilled, mental or physical – is the source of all value in human society. It is not machines, money, stocks or forces of supply and demand but, in the final analysis, productive human labour that is the source of all wealth. For Marx, this was not an emotive declaration but one backed by rigorous analysis. And by placing that role onto a broader segment of the population instead of on the genius of a few entrepreneurs, he converted economics into a profoundly humanistic discipline. In comparison, modern bourgeois economics, driven by arcane mathematical models whose meaning even the experts cannot explain and whose practical and predictive utility is strongly in doubt, is founded on amoral, elitist, profit-loss propositions that are fast driving the human race towards a global catastrophe. Rodney, to his credit, adopted the economic theory based on logic, fact and humanistic morality.

Those who judge the Marxist method simply based on documents produced by ossified political parties have an axe to grind. Taking a broader look, it is evident that this method is versatile enough to accurately capture the essence together with the specificities of diverse, complex social and economic realities. Far from being a rigid method, it has ample latitude for linking facts to interpretation in a diversity of ways.

The dominant bourgeois ideology functions to confound and conceal the economic reality of capitalism and imperialism. An attempt to bring it into the open, especially when it also deals with the immediate past and the present situation, encounters a barrage of shrill charges from multiple influential quarters, academic, media based and political. And no matter how often the charges are shown to be without a foundation, they are repeated *ad nauseam* as gospel truth. *HEUA* has regularly been a prime target of such an unfounded, politically motivated tendency.

## EXTERNAL FACTORS

Another oft aired criticism of *HEUA* is that it explains all the slave trade and post-slave trade era transformations in Africa by attaching the principal, if not the sole, importance to external forces and actors.

It is true that *HEUA* takes capitalism as an international system and views imperialism as basically an economically driven phenomenon. Though it notes the associated political, military, cultural and social components as well. The structures of external dependency established in the dominated nations and the resultant class structure constitute the pillars of imperial domination. Evolving over time, they facilitate extraction of the economic surplus from the dominated nation to the dominant nation, from lower classes to the upper classes, and underpin other forms of domination.

Imperialism fosters underdevelopment. But that does not imply absence of economic expansion. It denotes the institution of processes and rules that organically link the local economy and society to entities and forces operating in external economies. Economic growth is not identical to economic development. The latter is not feasible without weakening the structures of dependency. Yet, the situation is not always static or one-sided. At some historic junctures, external dependency notwithstanding, internal factors and struggles play a critical, and at times, a decisive role in efforts to transform the local social and economic conditions.

Rodney accords central importance to imperialism as the driver of the stupendous transformation in Africa in the past five centuries in the light of the extensive evidence he has marshalled. Currently, most historians accept his stand, at least as far as the end of the colonial era. Additional evidence from recent research shows that his thesis still remains as, if not more, valid.

Major differences arise when that thesis is extended to the post-colonial period. In that case, it is vigorously opposed by influential African and Western scholars. As if by a miracle, Western nations stand in a different relation to Africa today. They are no longer exploiters but aid givers and development guiders. There is economic malfeasance, for sure. But it is rare, and is due to some unscrupulous companies. It is not systemic in nature. The thesis of economic imperialism is not only factually flawed but also amounts to finding external scapegoats for Africa's present day maladies. They argue that it is time to stop pointing fingers at others and recognize that Africans, especially the corrupt, tyrannical leaders, bear the main responsibility for the state of turmoil and blocked progress in Africa. They point out that words like imperialism are conveniently used by autocrats like Mugabe to justify their failures.

Underdevelopment, in that view, is seen primarily as a state of mind. Africa remains backward because of lack of political will, local initiative, creativity and sustained effort. It is held that things can turn around dramatically if African people get their act together, hold their leaders to account, and embrace the spirit of entrepreneurship (Abdulazeez 2014; Mills 2011). Western nations have showered Africa with millions of dollars of assistance in education, health and social services. But the greedy leaders have squandered or stashed away the bounty given in good faith. Hence it remains a continent mired in destitution, conflict and despair. The key prescriptions for progress from the reigning school of thought include economic liberalization, promotion of local and foreign private investments, partnership between the private and public sectors, expanding exports, efficient utilization of foreign aid and a rapid expansion of the education sector. The high levels of GDP growth experienced by many African nations in the recent years are taken as indicators of the validity of this neoliberal strategy.

Yet, such voices are hardly new; they were heard in the early days of the Independence era too. Coming from influential quarters like the World Bank and the IMF, what they said was faithfully followed, within the specificities of the time, by most African nations. But it was this economic strategy that in large measure led to where Africa finds itself today. While a few elites within and beyond the continent benefitted immensely, the masses remained mired in endemic poverty. Whole regions and nations were destabilized at the core, and ripped apart by the violent convulsions whose roots lay in the economic and political brutality from above, grinding misery, unbearable pain, and frustrations that persisted for decades. Not a single nation in Africa, even one which had formed a political alliance with the socialist block, adopted a firm policy of disengagement from international capitalism. None sought to dismantle the structures of dependency. None took more than a few superficial measures to orient the economy onto a socialist path. These were the prerequisites for genuine development declared by Rodney. All thereby became mired in deep indebtedness to the West, and spiraled into catastrophic crises. That fate of post-Independence Africa does not negate Rodney's theory of structural dependency. Rather, it reveals the predictive power of the theory (Danaher 1994).

Rodney divided the then politically independent nations of Africa into two basic categories; a majority including Kenya and Nigeria that were ensconced within the neo-colonial orbit and a few like Tanzania that had declared a policy intended to discard the shackles of dependency. The University of Dar es Salaam was the canter of a vibrant debate on the theory and practice of the national policy of

Socialism and Self-Reliance adopted in 1967. Innovative investigations and astute socio-economic analysis by radical Tanzanian and expatriate scholars like Issa Shivji, Henry Mapolu, Justinian Rweyemamu, Adhu Awiti, Michela von Freyhold, Andrew Coulson and others indicated that despite impressive declarations of promoting self-reliance, Tanzania went on to adopt World bank supported policies that enhanced dependency rather than weaken it. The policy of *Ujamma* (cooperative socialism) came, in practice, to signify the establishment of a dependent, neo-colonial form of state capitalism rather than socialism.

Rodney was a key participant in this debate. But, at the outset, he did not concur with this viewpoint. In conjunction with scholars like John Saul, CLR James, and Lionel Cliffe, he felt that all was not lost. There was room for hope. However, after engaging with the local reality at the student, media, school and village levels, Rodney's viewpoint evolved while that of most arm-chair leftist academics tended to remain static. By the mid-1970s, he had recognized that the rhetoric socialism masked the reality of neo-colonial dependency being implemented by a petty bourgeois bureaucracy. The point is that he was both a Marxist scholar and a committed activist, continually enhancing his perspective through study and struggle (Hirji 2011;2013; Shivji 2012). (see also Chapter 9).

Today, he would remind us that those entities who once openly backed dictators and robbers in Africa, whose companies exploited Africa's mineral and other resources to the last ounce without producing any long-term benefits for Africa, the same actors are reborn as promoters and funders of welfare, human rights and good governance for the people of Africa. He would note that the picture of Africa rising painted by such sources is a fairy tale, a distorted half-truth. Scores of studies document the continued exploitation of African economies by external actors; that what is extracted from Africa far exceeds what is brought in by aid, investments, etc.; that the terms of trade for Africa remain adverse; that African economies are dangerously captive to unstable external market forces; that it is mostly the local elite, wealthy business class and foreign investors who reap the whirlwind; that excessive economic inequality and complete lack of accountability are the norm; that state resources are regularly diverted to serve local elites and foreign entities; and so on.

Ample documentation of how neo-liberal policies operate in Africa today exists. The nature of their impact on the economic, political and social fronts is also known. Suffice to say that Africa is undergoing, in a new form, the very process of development of underdevelopment exposed by Rodney. Dependency and servitude on all fronts are on the upswing. More and more, the outside powers call the shots, right to the micro level; and even militarily, Africa is coming under the purview of the US. More billionaires are born in Africa than ever before, yet the levels of poverty and childhood malnutrition remain stubbornly high. The growth and social progress seen are temporary and of the superficial kind. A few years of export driven economic euphoria are followed by business closures, a major burden of national debt and mass unemployment in the formal and informal sectors of the economy. The cases of South Africa, Ghana, Ethiopia, Kenya and Uganda illustrate this tendency. Once heralded as leaders in development, they now face mounting economic crises (Burgis 2015).

In comparison to Rodney's era, the particulars have changed. The presence of China makes the picture more complex. Yet, his structural elucidation of the African condition retains its validity and relevance. And so does his method of historic analysis.

Today, he would tell us to abandon the binary local-external viewpoint and realize that it is the alliance between the locally dominant economic class, local political elite, imperial states and multinational firms that lie at the root of Africa's predicament. Neo-liberalism, he would proclaim, is the highest stage of neo-colonialism.

When talking of economic imperialism, establishment pundits, scholars and media usually make one exception. As far as Chinese investments and assistance in Africa are concerned, they find no compunction in applying that idea. China is castigated in an automatic manner of harboring imperial designs. Unfortunately, most African scholars repeat that ideologically driven tirade as well.

The actions of China in Africa do have imperialistic aspects. But that is not the issue here. I am simply pointing out a blatant double standard. It has also to be kept in mind that China operates within the confines of a global capitalist system instituted by Western powers, whose rules are enforced by agencies they dominate, and which is ultimately protected by the US military with its over 1,000 bases spread across the globe (Burgis 2015; Editor 2015; Foster 2006; Vine 2015; Wolf 2014).

## DENIAL OF AGENCY

The charge of converting the history of Africa into a process solely determined by, and for the exclusive interest of, external forces engendered a complementary, frequently aired complaint against *HEUA*: that it *denies agency* to the people of Africa; that it portrays them as incapable of making their own history; and that their valiant actions and remarkable achievements in countering the external forces are seriously downplayed if not ignored altogether. It is hence alleged that Rodney converted Africans into pawns of external parties and economic forces.

I reflect upon the substance and implications of this serious accusation at three distinct levels: personal, strategic and historiographical.

Rodney was an activist and a revolutionary *par excellence*. Grounding with his brothers and radical scholarship got him expelled from Jamaica. In Tanzania, he worked closely with the radical students at the University of Dar es Salaam; was intimately involved in the struggles to convert the orientation of the course curricula from a bourgeois one into a socialist one; lived and worked in *Ujamaa* (cooperative villages); regularly spoke on socio-political topics in secondary schools and colleges; supported in words and deeds, the African, Palestinian, African-American and Vietnamese struggles; wrote articles on burning issues of the day in the popular media and gave public lectures at the university campus on a frequent basis. Denounced by Western embassies, he now and then also landed in trouble with the university and state authorities. At home in Guyana, he became a full-time revolutionary and was in the collective leadership of the Working Peoples Alliance, a radical political movement whose aim was to replace the exploitative neo-colonial order with a just and racially harmonious society. And he was killed in the trenches.

Consequently, Rodney embodied, in flesh, blood and spirit, the very idea of historic agency. He did not wait for automatic forces, economic or otherwise, to initiate societal transformation. Instead, he mobilized and worked for a better future for Africa, the Caribbean and humanity. On the personal level, the charge of denial of agency levied against Rodney is a patently absurd charge.

It is one thing to fight for change, but quite another to have an effective strategy to bring it about. Radicalism flounders if it is not grounded in a strategy that takes into account the major forces blocking change, and has a valid perspective for long term transformation. The fate of the recent Arab Spring uprisings testifies to that proposition. Those popular movements did not take Western imperialism, the class nature of state power and the economic dimension into account. Not surprisingly, in a short while, the nation minus the former dictator either landed into a condition of utter chaos, or returned to the same or worse form of the neoliberal quagmire.

Rodney's investigations into history aimed to unearth the forces blocking change and those that would propel the change in the desired direction. By aiming to provide the people with effective theoretical tools for their struggles, he was not only cognizant as to the primacy of their agency but also desired to enhance the possibility of successful outcomes in their struggles. As he put it:

[E]very African has the responsibility to understand the [imperialist] system and work for its overthrow (*HEUA*, p 28).

Thus, on the political and strategic fronts, calling Rodney a denier of agency is a meaningless charge.

On the historiographical level, the question of agency pertains to writing of history that fully accounts for the actions of all the strata of society that figure in that process, both in times of stability and times of major change. For colonial Africa, we can divide the actions of the colonized people into four main phases: (i) resistance against the imposition and expansion of rule by the imperial forces; (ii) adapting to an established colonial order; (iii) acting at the individual and group levels to improve life conditions but within the confines of the colonial order; and (iv) mobilizing and acting on a nationwide basis to banish colonial rule. The stratagem of divide and rule, and historic relations between different communities in the colony implied that all communities did not react uniformly. Some cooperated with the rulers, others stridently opposed them. This lent complexity to the question of elucidating agency.

Let us explore the issue through his own words. In the first place:

Africans everywhere fought against alien political rule, and had to be subdued by superior force (*HEUA*, p 141).

Consequently, a new order emerged in Africa:

[U]nder colonialism, power lay in the hands of the colonialists. …. Colonialism was a negation of freedom from the viewpoint of the colonized (*HEUA*, p 223).

Nonetheless, the people of Africa did not lapse into passivity, resigned to the overwhelming power exercised by their rulers.

Within any social system, the oppressed find some room to maneuver through their own initiative (*HEUA*, p 223).

Giving several instances of this type of efforts in colonial Africa, he marvels at

the tremendous vigour displayed by Africans in mastering the principles of the system that had mastered them (*HEUA*, 263).

Nonetheless, such struggles for improvement within the colonial order were not the end of the game for the people. They eventually embarked on the path to full self-determination. As Rodney aptly expresses it:

> True historical initiative by a whole people or by individuals requires that they have the power to decide the *direction* in which they want to move (*HEUA*, pp 222—222).

Upon observing the successful outcomes of these struggles, Rodney counters the views of those who claim that Independence was granted to Africa on a silver platter.

> It should be emphasized that the choice that Africa should be free was not made by the colonial powers but by the people of Africa (*HEUA*, p 259).

Political independence, though a crucial, essential step in the struggle for liberation came with basic limitations. The shackles of imperial domination, especially on the economic front, largely persisted. Rodney thus points towards continued struggle by the people of Africa. Taking the example of Cameroon, he ends his book by recognizing and advocating

> the element of *conscious activity* that signifies the ability to make history by grappling with the heritage of objective material conditions and social relations. (*HEUA*, p 280).

It is abundantly evident that Rodney is cognizant of the centrality of popular agency in African history and of the need to express it clear terms. Across the pages of *HEUA*, he gives instances of all the four levels of agency under colonial rule and notes their contradictory features. The matter is brought into prominence at the end of the book when he analyses the role of education during colonialism.

However, what Rodney can be taken to task for is not covering the issue of resistance in greater depth anywhere in the book. For example, it lacks details about the nature and course of anti-colonial movements and struggles in different parts of Africa.

But there was specific reason for that. Rodney did not set out to write a general history of Africa. Rather, he wanted an inexpensive, accessible, short work to explain in plain English what the title of the book stated. *HEUA* was written at a time when the economic reality of colonial domination was an almost taboo topic in the general African history texts. He managed to bring the issue to the forefront to an extent that in a few years it became an unavoidable thing to mention, even for the mainstream historians.

The charge of short changing agency on the historiographical front is thus a charge that stems from ignoring the aims of the author. It does not reflect a methodological limitation on his part. Those who make that claim seem to have read his book in a distinctively superficial manner. And despite the limitation of illustrations about popular struggles, given the thousands of students, activists and people he educated and inspired into action, he practically enhanced agency in a major way.

One other point about denial of agency is often overlooked. It seems logical that whenever one posits an extraneous force as a driving force of history, one, to an extent, reduces human agency from history. For example, some modern historians assert that environmental factors have been the main determinants of African history. Why are they not accused of denying agency to the people? Why are they not critiqued for reducing Africans to be blind victims of environmental forces?

Additionally, the question of agency is a two-way affair. In the period he covers, there were contradictions between classes, political groups and nations within Europe that affected the nature and course of European interventions in Africa. It was not a matter of a monolithic Europe, led by automatic laws of capitalist development, driven to impose hegemony over a monolithic Africa. Yet, Rodney covers the intra-European contradictions to an even smaller degree. One wonders why those who brand him a denier of agency to the people of Africa do not as well brand him a denier of agency to the people of Europe.

Furthermore, those who uphold the notion African agency surprisingly have little compunction in surrendering the fate of Africa today into the hands of external entities – the foreign 'donors', investors and banks. They are treated as the indispensable saviors of the unstable, badly governed nations of Africa. Rodney, however, would expose them as the exploiters of Africa who bear a major responsibility for its current problems. Hence the difference lies not so much in the relative emphasis placed on external entities but in how they are perceived—benefactors or bandits?

The final point is that social struggles derive from the social relations. On the latter issue, it is hard to fault Rodney. At all the stages of the historic process he writes on, he takes into account the relations between the existent or evolving groups and classes in society, in Africa and Europe, and addresses their interconnections. Open a page at random in his book and you will likely find a relevant example. While *HEUA* lacks details on social struggles, it does adequately depict the social relations connected with the development of underdevelopment.

**POLEMICAL STYLE**

Academic writing for any discipline is expected to use the discipline-specific terminology, and be, as well as appear to be, unbiased. It is expected to avoid emotive phrases, exaggeration and prejudicial terms.

Works of history correspondingly must be scientific expositions that reflect dispassionate objectivity. That is the traditional academic lore.

At first sight, in *HEUA*, Rodney seems to have dispensed with these norms. It is thereby castigated as a polemical, unscholarly work. For example, instead of denoting the Africans who sided with the colonizers in neutral terms – say, internal facilitators of colonial rule – he calls them stooges, a pejorative label. Collins and Burns (2007) reflect the mainstream view as they denigrate the book for its 'polemical' and 'inflammatory' tone. It is implied that the presence of such features calls the author's objectivity into question.

Yet, we note a double standard here. Mainstream American historians have no qualms about calling their country folk who supported the British in the war for independence turncoats. But such a label used in the African context, particularly when it is directed against Western powers or interests, suddenly becomes a no-no.

At the root of this criticism lies the key issue of the relationship between style and substance. The case of research papers published in prominent medical journals in the US and UK over the past two decades provides a valuable insight into that issue. Editorial rules require that the layout of these papers follow a standard structure, and avoid emotive, colorful, or subjective terminology. Only hard facts, scientific methodology and logical interpretations are allowed. An anonymous system of peer-review guards against the violation of these hallowed rules.

Yet, despite apparent adherence to such standards, these journals have been repeatedly embroiled in scandals involving publication of biased, unethical, substance-wise and methodologically deficient, and yes, plainly fraudulent research. Senior professors and researchers from leading US, British, European and Asian universities featured as the authors of these flawed papers. Research funded by drug and medical companies had a higher probability of being tainted with such bias. The recommendations stemming from them had higher risks of inflicting harm on patients. It was only due to a series of lawsuits, and efforts of whistle blowers and astute investigators that the ugly truth began to come to light. Many journals have reacted to the scandals by adopting strict rules about registration of health studies at the outset, declaration of conflict of interest, instilling transparency in research, data sharing, data reanalysis, and so on. Yet, one or the other scandal of this form continues to surface now and then. Of the hundreds of work dealing with this topic, see Angell (2005), Chan et al (2004), DeAngelis (2000;2006), Editorial (2004;2006), Hirji (2009), Hirji and Premji (2011), Kassirer (2000), Lewis (2010); Mayer (2005) and Moore (1995).

An objective type of writing style is far from a guarantee against egregious one-sidedness. By resorting to effusive, scientifically sounding terminology, protocol deviations, data selectivity, unnecessarily complex techniques of analysis and a convoluted, minimally informative style of presentation, modern day researchers have mastered the art of slanting research conclusions in a desired direction. But, on the surface, the style seems objective and neutral. Intense competition for research funding, diminished academic autonomy, the publish-or-perish culture, corporate inroads into the academia and computerization have enhanced such practices. Having a strongly worded writing style in this environment is among the least of the concerns.

One should not conflate style with substance. The merits of a non-fiction book should be assessed based on its methodology, inner logic, and content, not just the style. At times, a conclusion based on valid research may, and rightfully so, be expressed in terms carrying moral undertones. Whistle-blowers and academics who uncover egregious violations of human welfare, and activists who stand up to unjust authorities often express indignation over what they have found. On the other hand, one should doubt the commitment to the truth on the part of the scholars who look the other way, and proceed with business as usual in such ethically compelling circumstances.

Walter Rodney wrote about a continent that had been misrepresented, devalued, and denigrated for centuries. Those portrayals had justified the subjugation and exploitation of its people. So, he did not mince words when characterizing that reality. If anything, he deserves praise for breaking the silence, and jarring the conscience of his colleagues.

Furthermore, what is deemed polemical depends on your point of view. Many Africa oriented scholars took the label 'underdeveloped' to be a demeaning label. It seemed to imply that Africans were incapable on their own of attaining development. Hence, they preferred the positive descriptor 'developing country' for an African nation.

Why did Rodney employ that negative descriptor? And if he had wanted to sensationalize the issues why not use titles and words like *How the White Man Plundered Africa*, or *How Europe Brutalized (Conned, Duped, Murdered) Africans and Fleeced (Denuded, Mangled, Pillaged, Razed, Vandalized) Their Economy and Society*, etc. Labels like *impoverished, fleeced, leeched, pauperized* or *ransacked* dispersed within the pages of the book would have enhanced its polemical flavour and increased its grassroots popularity.

Yet, Rodney almost monotonously stuck to one sedate descriptor. Why? In his parlance, *underdevelopment* was not a vague, vilifying term. It was a carefully formulated socio-economic concept underpinned by a large body of analytic works. *HEUA* begins with a detailed explanation of this and related terms. As employed there, *underdevelopment* is neither an emotive nor a polemical adjective.

What the establishment academics dub polemical and what they do not reflects ideologically driven double standards. Consider, for example, the discussion of proliferation of intensely violent conflicts in Africa in the recent decades given in Reid (2012). Among the most important causes stated is the 'massive influx ... of automatic weapons, and in particular the increasingly ubiquitous AK-47' (p 333). Only the Eastern-Bloc nations are explicitly mentioned here. While establishment historians take a statement of this sort as a neutrally framed, objective statement of fact, in reality it is anything but. Persistent repetition in the Western media has made it appear so. But an investigation of the militarization of Africa reveals it to be a biased declaration. Media bias entrenches and elicits an emotive response: Yes, the communists were the primary, if not the sole, source of violence in Africa in those days. In singing this song, the systematic, regular and massive support given by the US and other Western nations to military dictatorships, military coups against civilian governments, right wing rebel groups, Apartheid and colonial regimes, and terrorist fighters is pushed under the rug. Objectively speaking, statements of the type quoted above are emotive, polemical statements that reflect at best a half truth.

If you dislike the message, shoot the messenger: this ancient practice is gaining momentum in these neo-liberal times. Writers of anti-corporate, anti-establishment, anti-imperial books are called on the carpet not for what have written, but for how they have expressed themselves. They are accused of violating the rules of civility and harmonious discourse. Their chances of promotion and tenure diminish; some face expulsion. Angela Davis was sanctioned at the University of California on similar spurious grounds (Scott 2015). The question of style is an effective tool to silence alternative voices.

Instead of critiquing what he actually wrote and engaging with Marxist historiography, Rodney's detractors take exception to particular terms or phrases. It leads to the claim that his book is biased and sensationalistic. But this claim too is devoid of merit.

## SCHOLARSHIP AND ACTIVISM

The traditional academic stand projects an ideal historian as a dispassionate investigator of societal change. Setting aside prejudice, politics, exaggeration and distortion, he or she focuses on uncovering and relating facts, just the facts. Activists of varied persuasions may infer socio-political messages from those facts. That, however, is not the business of the historian. In particular, he/she should desist from injecting politics and agitation into the academy.

Colin and Burns (2007) state that *HEUA* was written to 'raise public awareness' about the colonial and on-going exploitation of Africa (p 310). The implication is that by mixing activism with scholarship, Rodney diluted its scholarly worth and turned it into a propaganda document.

But that judgement derives from a misrepresentation of the actuality of historical research and writing. No history text is just a neutral collection of facts. Explicitly or implicitly, each historical work is propelled by a theory, is infused with values, and incorporates a socio-economic perspective. These entities are embedded within it through varied mechanisms, subtle or overt. The research process is as well tainted by these factors.

As summarized by Mamdani (2012), the historian Yusuf Bala Usman has well captured the essence of the linkage between history and objectivity:

> It is ... impossible to reconstruct history without having specific categories, conception and assumption. What is suggested here is that unless this is done consciously one becomes a conceptual prisoner of certain types of primary sources without being aware of it. Bala Usman quoted in Mamdani (2012), p 91.

Renditions of the past project judgements of the present and the *future*. And they do so from the perspective and interests of specific social groups, social systems or nations. A work claiming to be purely objective camouflages an implicit endorsement of the existing social order. It depicts the dominant social values and norms as natural, sacrosanct, unchangeable entities, and is suffused with unscientific notions that people take for granted in the same way as they do the air they are breathing. The next chapter has specific instances of this phenomenon: All the eight mainstream books reviewed there are shown to be ultimately biased towards the currently prevailing neoliberal ideology.

The difference between Marxist and other historians is thereby not in the presence of values, premises and social orientation but in their nature. Marxists declare their theory and values openly; others hide behind an artificial shroud of scholarly impartiality. Every historian is an activist; the question is whether one is a pro-*status quo* activist, or an activist who questions the foundation of the existing social order (Swai 1981;1982: Zinn 1990).

Rodney was the second type of activist. He did not artificially separate scholarship and activism or effusively claim to be above society. Instead, in a mark of his intellectual integrity, he openly declared the theory, ethics and orientation he espoused. Nonetheless, as he sought to inspire and mobilize for the liberation of Africa, he did not compromise his methodological rigor or short change facts.

Some mainstream historians practice plainly unethical activism openly. In the Cold War era, many US historians were funded by the CIA or the US military. Presently, several Africa oriented US historians and their African colleagues obtain research funds from AFRICOM, the US military command for Africa (for example, see the Minerva Project shown at http://minerva.dtic.mil). Others practice pro-establishment activism by ignoring or minimizing the injustice and outrageous deeds perpetrated by 'their side' but disproportionately highlighting those of the 'other side.' Silence becomes a tacit endorsement of injustice, an unethical brand of activism.

Activism is also associated with how one interprets the idea of agency. Many mainstream historians, including Afrocentric historians for whom it is the key point, interpret it at the level of policy makers and the political elite, especially when one deals with the post-Independence era. They direct their gaze at existent political structures, corporate board rooms, wealthy foundations, NGOs and official institutions. They seek reforms, but within the system. On the other hand, Rodney, as the totality of his life and writings show, interpreted the idea at the level of the masses. His main goal, in the academia and beyond, was to empower ordinary people to enable them to determine their own destiny. Were he alive today, he would be exposing the exploitative reality of neoliberalism, and castigating imperialists and their local stooges in public forums. He would tell us not to place reliance of externally funded NGOs and human rights organizations but to develop grassroots mass movements. And he would not just tell us, he would be deeply immersed in those struggles and be a leading activist organizing for fundamental social change as well. That is the key reason why establishment historians judge him harshly and unfairly. By showing solidarity with the masses instead of the elites, he exposed their self-serving biases and put them to shame.

And that is why they subject him to a double standard. Take John Iliffe, a top-of-the-ladder historian. He begins his widely used text, *Africans: The History of a Continent*, by stating that Africa's 'contemporary problems [and] situation' constitute the 'purpose' and 'organizing theme' of the book (Iliffe 2007). Grandiose declarations to influence some change in society is a common practice. It is a form of activism. But when Rodney makes such a declaration, he is pilloried to no end.

On the one hand, he is branded a denier of agency, and on the other, he is blamed for being a political activist, that is, a practitioner of agency in its clearest form. But one needs to judge him from his own plainly expressed views. Talking of his overall perspective on underdevelopment, he tells us:

> None of these remarks are intended to remove the ultimate responsibility for development on the shoulders Africans (*HEUA*, p 29).

## BLACK NATIONALISM AND PSEUDO-MARXISM

Interestingly, Rodney has faced strong criticism from left-wing circles too. Their main gripe is that *HEUA* so much underplays internal class relations and struggles that it cannot be deemed a work of Marxist political economy. The rhetoric of the book, it is said, is more in line with racially oriented black nationalism than with a socialistic outlook.

The philosophy of a genuine scholar evolves over the course of his or her life. Initially, Walter Rodney emerged in a milieu in which nationalism of a racial variety was popular among the anti-colonial activists. He was concurrently also mentored by eminent Marxists like CLR James. His philosophical evolution was characterized by tension between these ideas. His involvement in the struggles on the ground, and theoretical studies came to affect which of them would ultimately prevail.

When Rodney landed at the University of Dar es Salaam, he faced these tendencies during his interactions with the radical students and lecturers, his work with the African liberation movements, his forays into university politics, and his practical and ideological-level involvements in Tanzania's policy of Socialism and Self-Reliance. These activities and his own theoretical endeavors decisively drew him steadily towards Marxism and away from a race or nationality based outlook.

By the time he wrote *HEUA*, he had adopted Marxism as his primary world outlook. The theoretical framework explained in Chapter 1 leaves us in no doubt about that. And throughout the book, his invective is directed not at persons, races or nationalities. His target is a social-economic system and the forces it nurtures. While his terminology is forthright, he does not blame entire races or nationalities. When necessary, he does not hesitate to criticize African social groups. But the basis of the criticism is the role played in facilitating colonial domination, and not any other feature. The essence of his view on race is given thus:

> Occasionally, it is mistakenly held that Europeans enslaved Africans for racist reasons. European miners and planters enslaved Africans for *economic* reasons, so that their labour power could be exploited. .. Then,

having become utterly dependent on African labour, Europeans at home and abroad found it necessary to rationalize that exploitation in racist terms as well. Oppression follows exploitation, so as to guarantee the latter. Oppression of African people on purely racial grounds accompanied, strengthened and became indistinguishable from oppression for economic reasons (*HEUA*, pp 88–89).

As Rodney posits the primacy of economics, he reminds us that racism has a momentum of its own, eventually making it a potent, independent force in society. This historically valid perspective is not appreciated by those who view issues in disjoint binary terms like race or class, race or economics, Marxism or nationalism.

Rodney's intellectual evolution continued all along. He actively participated in the vibrant debate on the characterization of the socialist policy being implemented in Tanzania. The campus community of radicals had major divisions on this issue. At the outset, he had an optimistic, nationalistic form of stand. Later, taking cognition of the reality of state capitalism, he became more critical. Yet, the views he expressed were all within the Marxist, socialist framework (see Chapter 9 for further details).

The tendency to ascribe racial types of motivation to Rodney persists. In part, that is due to the differences he had over issues like curriculum reform with the progressive European and North American academics at the university. Rodney was more aware of the local sensitivity towards external meddling in local affairs. At times, such sensitivity masked a retrogressive, anti-socialistic line. But as an outsider himself, he had to strike a balance. He respected the right of Tanzanians to chart their own future, and resented the know-all scholars from the West who tended to prescribe their own pet programs without contextual considerations. On occasion, he sided with the local staff even as other progressive colleagues felt that it was a questionable stand. Labelling Rodney as a racially biased person stems to a large degree from the continued circulation of stories about such incidents.

In his popular writings, Rodney wrote in a fiercely forthright style. It is easy to quote them selectively to show that he was a racist. For example, in Chapter 6 of *The Groundings with My Brothers*, he writes '… all white people are enemies until proved otherwise…' Taken by itself, this line leads to one conclusion. But if you read what follows as well: 'all white people are enemies until proved otherwise and this applies to black intellectuals, all of us are enemies to the people until we prove otherwise,' you see that for Rodney blackness and whiteness are not biologic entities but sociologic constructs emerging from a racist colonial system (Rodney 2014, p 58). When he talks of white racism in

*HEUA*, he is describing a concrete historical phenomenon whereby the alleged cultural, intellectual and moral superiority of Europeans was used to enslave, colonize, demean and brutalize Africans.

It is wholly incorrect label Rodney a racist. He treated humans as humans. At the personal, professional or political level, he was a firm anti-racist.

There are also Marxists who question his Marxism but on other grounds. They say he did not comprehend the nature and import of internal class divisions and struggles. Instead, he adopted the dependency theory framework that is too economistic and structural.

As noted earlier, Rodney was cognizant of the importance of internal class relations and social struggles. He dealt with the former in an adequate manner and but did not go into details about the latter in *HEUA*. This was because he did not set out to write a broad history of Africa. He had a specific focus, which was to explicate in clear terms a crucial dimension of that history that had been grossly hidden and distorted until then.

The purist Marxists brand anything that does not follow what they deem the true Marxist line as anti-Marxist. With a narrow conceptual horizon, they are unaware that Marxism is not a monolithic intellectual entity. Like any field of science, it has extensive room for debate. It is not a religion. A single, correct Marxist line does not exist. Those who seek to banish Rodney from the community of Marxists on such grounds only display their shallow understanding of Marxism.

This criticism can be seen as the obverse of the charge that he denied agency to the people of Africa. What has been said above on the question of agency also applies here. This issue is further addressed in the next chapter.

### THE WOMAN QUESTION

Modern day feminists would critique Rodney for failing to recognize the central role of women in African history, their subjugation in pre-European contact and subsequent periods, and the role they played in the liberation struggles.

Yet, he does lay down his basic position on these issues. In the colonial context, for example, he indicates:

> The colonialists in Africa occasionally paid lip service to women's education and emancipation, but objectively there was deterioration in the status of women owing to colonial rule (*HEUA*, p 226).

This statement arises in a one-page discussion of the dual nature – traditional, familial and colonially derived – of women's oppression. In the final chapter, he gives details on the few educational opportunities available to African women under colonialism. He notes that educational avenues open for them, especially beyond the primary level, were fewer than the pitiful avenues available to African men.

Rodney does not elaborate on the role of women in confronting imperial rule for the same reason as why he does not give a detailed picture of anti-imperialist struggles in general, the varied character African political movements, the role of different ethnicities, the importance of cultural tools, etc. While noting his basic positions on such matters, he remains focused on the central theme of his book, namely, elucidating with clarity and in unimpeachable terms, the development of underdevelopment in Africa.

Rodney was a firm supporter of women's liberation. Yet, he would also critique the present-day promoters of women's rights in Africa for their high degree of reliance on funding from Western sources and pursuing agendas that remains squarely within the confines of the neo-liberal order, an order that imposes mighty barriers against autonomous, significant progress for the people of Africa, including the women of Africa.

## FACTUAL ERRORS

While the *History of the Upper Guinea Coast* is a strikingly original work in terms of factual contents and method, the novelty of *HEUA* lies in how Rodney synthesized a large body of existing work within the political economy framework. He ventured further than any earlier attempt to produce a comprehensive narrative that was simultaneously consistent and persuasive. He highlighted known but hitherto neglected material, reinterpreted what was written earlier and enjoined apparently disparate facts and issues. A good example is his astute presentation of the multi-faceted nature of education under colonial rule.

However, since *HEUA* was written, an extensive volume of research on African history — archival, excavation-based, oral and genetic — has been done. Examining the book from the current vantage point would surely reveal deficiencies and errors of fact that need to be rectified. For example, there have been contentions about the accuracy of the volume of slave traffic given in the book. Some researchers claimed it was too high while others said it was in the right ball park range. Other socio-economic data covering the colonial period may need rectification as well.

On the other hand, a growing body on newly unearthed findings reveals that the brutality, calculated deviousness and economic depredations of the colonial rulers went further than what Rodney depicts. This applies to the actions of Belgium in the Congo, the British in Kenya, the Germans in Botswana, the French in Algeria and elsewhere and, notoriously, of the Portuguese in Angola and Mozambique. Even in a trust territory like Tanganyika, the British blatantly violated the UN requirements to prepare the territory for independence and tried, through pugnacious tactics, to maintain an Apartheid-like societal situation and control for as long as practicable and politically feasible. For elucidation see Anderson (2013), Cobain (2012), Elkins (2005), Grandin (2011), Hochschild (1999), Klein (2008), Lindqvist (1997), Mukerjee (2011), Perkins (2006), Prashad (2007), Wolf (2014) and Wright and Reilly (2011).

A crucial observation made in *HEUA* was that colonial massacres formed a backdrop for, and were effectively, training grounds for fascist genocides in Europe. This thesis was investigated systematically and given solid credence by Lindqvist (1997).

Taking such recent findings into account, Rodney could rewrite without a modicum of doubt precisely what he had done earlier: 'The only good thing about colonialism was when it ended.' I posit that the findings of modern historic research, more than anything else, reveal the depth of his historic insight.

Were he alive, Rodney would have brought out an expanded, corrected edition of his book. Yet, and what is important, his framework for approaching history and his primary conclusions would not only remain essentially the same as before but could be presented with greater confidence.

It has now been clearly established that as the day of Independence drew closer, colonial powers went to great lengths to hide the reality of their rule. It was a centrally directed, massive and systematic exercise to destroy or transfer to the home country literally tons of official documents. This was complemented by doctoring the files left in place in such a way as to paint colonial rule as a benign and benevolent process (Cobain 2016; Jack 2016).

Yet, colonial rule was a horrifyingly brutal and consciously rapacious enterprise, a crime against humanity. The same holds for the American actions in Africa in that era. But these misdeeds were hidden from the future generations with the complicity of the major media and venerated scholars from those nations. Rodney was aware of the biased and incomplete nature of the official documents and the mainstream narratives. In the light of what has come to surface of recent, it is not he but the plethora of so-called objective historians who almost blindly relied on the official story and gave us a distorted version of African history who need to go back to the drawing board and produce significantly revised versions of their books and papers. And they, who perpetually bemoan Stalinist censorship of the past, have to be on the forefront of the movement for full disclosure of the true story of colonial rule in Africa, much of which remains hidden in imperial vaults.

## AN OVERALL VERDICT

The above discussion of the charges that have been levelled against *HEUA* leads me to draw the following conclusions:

1. The charge that it converts African history into a rigid deterministic process arising from external economic relations, and so denies agency to the people of Africa, has no validity. It is an ideologically driven claim without a substantive basis.
2. The charge that it is a work of political propaganda, of the Marxist or black nationalistic variety, and thus lacking in scholarly worth is also a charge without credibility.
3. The charge that it is written in an emotive, polemical style can only arise upon a failure to understand the well-defined, empirically grounded and consistently deployed terminology used in the book.
4. While the book pays due attention to internal social and class relations, it is wanting in terms of depiction of internal social, class, anti-colonial and anti-imperial struggles. But that is because it was not meant to portray the general history of Africa. It had a specific focus. This deficiency does not reflect a methodological flaw or an oversight on the part of the author.
5. The voluminous research in African history that has done since its publication has brought forth new material that will help correct some errors of fact and interpretation in the book. However, a large portion of the new material confirms, not negates, the basic thesis of *HEUA*. Such errors are inevitable for any long-standing work, however accurate it may have been deemed in the past.

Walter Rodney was certainly not the first historian to apply the Marxist method to unravel the history of Africa. But he was the most influential one. His approach to history was not that of an accountant producing a balance sheet. Instead, he adopted a systemic method that sought to unveil, within an interdisciplinary perspective, the short and long term dynamics of societal change in Africa. It did not blame races, nations or religions but looked for explanations within the framework of an evolving global capitalist system, the tentacles it had spread in Africa, and the consequences for the people.

The dominant bourgeois ideology functions to confound and conceal the economic reality of capitalism and imperialism. An attempt to bring it into the open encounters a barrage of shrill charges from influential quarters, academic, media based and political. And no matter how often the charges are shown to be without a foundation, they are repeated *ad nauseam* as gospel truth. That is a major reason why *HEUA* has been a prime target of such an unfounded, politically motivated tendency. In sum, most of the charges against *HEUA* are automatic, politically motivated criticisms.

Notwithstanding the tirades of the apologists of neo-liberalism, it retains its worth as a paradigm shifting work of history that seamlessly enjoins sound scholarship with astute activism. Its methodology is as indispensable today as it was at the time it came out. Written in an inspirational style, it brims with deep historic and projective insights. This prescient work remains a sturdy guide in the struggles for progressive social transformation in Africa and beyond.

The conclusions I state here are supported by the findings of the survey of eight classroom texts on the history of Africa given in Chapter 7. The long-term influence of the political economy based approach of *HEUA* in such texts is hard to miss. At least into the colonial era, most of them now accord due weight to economic issues and the deleterious aspects of external economic linkages. Nevertheless, they rarely directly acknowledge that influence, and when they explicitly refer to Rodney or his works, they do so in a biased and distorted manner.

A fuller understanding of Rodney's historical method and insights requires reading *HEUA* as well as his *History of the Upper Guinea Coast, 1540 to 1800*. Proceeding through both these books, the reader may reflect on the criticisms noted above, and draw his or her own conclusions. A comparison with the responses I have given will constitute an illuminating pedagogic journey.

## Chapter 7

## RODNEY IN THE CLASSROOM

With the general expunging of anti-capitalist texts from education, the use of *HEUA* in courses in African history in universities of Africa, Europe and the Americas has waned considerably. Once upon a time, all undergraduates at the University of Dar es Salaam were exposed to it. Today, a student at the same institution can attain a bachelor's degree in history without having read it from cover to cover. At best, students learn about its contents in a second-hand manner.

This gives rise several concerns: Is *HEUA* still referenced in the general textbooks on African history? Do they incorporate aspects of the political-economy strand of historiography? Do they provide an adequate and fair picture of Rodney's contribution to African history?

Quite a few general African history books, new and revised versions, are currently available. Books with an avowedly Afrocentric orientation are few, and those with a Marxist framework are a rarity. Most books derive from the nationalistic, Africanist approach. But these do not have a uniform methodology. Their sub-strands emanate from the key factors they utilize to explain historical change. These factors include the environment, population, economy, culture, gender, ethnic relations, governance, religion and socio-political relations.

For the purpose of getting a handle on the queries posed above, I selected eight books with a continental horizon that are in use in African history classes today:

1. Asante MK (2007) *The History of Africa* (new edition), Routledge, New York.
2. Collins RO and Burns JM (2007) *A History of Sub-Saharan Africa*, Cambridge University Press, Cambridge, UK.
3. Freund B (1998) *The Making of Contemporary Africa: The*

*Development of African Society since 1800* (second edition), Palgrave Macmillan, UK.
4. Iliffe J (2007) *Africans: The History of a Continent* (second edition), Cambridge University Press, Cambridge, UK.
5. Laumann D (2012) *Colonial Africa: 1884–1994 (African World Histories)*, Oxford University Press, Oxford.
6. Reader J (1999) *Africa: A Biography of the Continent*, Vintage, New York.
7. Reid RJ (2012) *A History of Modern Africa: 1800 to the Present* (second edition), Wiley-Blackwell, New York.
8. Shillington K (2012) *History of Africa* (third edition), Palgrave-MacMillan, New York.

I begin by listing the references to Rodney and his two main works, *HEUA* and *History of the Upper Guinea Coast (HUGC)*, in the text, text notes, references and recommended readings, and the Index. The result is tabulated below (note: Other(s) = Work(s) of Rodney other than *HEUA* or *HUGC*).

| Book | References | Text & Notes | Index |
| --- | --- | --- | --- |
| **Asante (2007)** | *HEUA* | Rodney (1) | Rodney (1) |
| **Collins and Burns (2007)** | *HEUA* + Other | *HEUA* (3) | Rodney (3) |
| **Freund B (1998)** | *HEUA* + Others | *HEUA* (2) | Rodney (2) |
| **Iliffe (2007)** | *HEUA* | *HEUA* (1) | None |
| **Laumann (2012)** | *HEUA* | *HEUA* (3) | Rodney (2) |
| **Reader (1999)** | *HEUA* + *HUGC* | *HEUA* (3) | None |
| **Reid (2012)** | None | None | None |
| **Shillington (2012)** | None | *HEUA* (3) | *HEUA* (2) |

Rodney has an explicit presence in seven of these eight textbooks. At first glance, we thus get the impression that his ideas continue to be conveyed, in one form or another, to students of African history. An in-depth look, however, reveals that the reality is much more convoluted. This is best seen by examining the books one at a time.

### ASANTE (2007)

In this premier work espousing the Afrocentric approach to African history, there is but a single reference to Walter Rodney. The book is dedicated to eight 'Fathers of African History.' Ali Mazrui is listed here but Rodney, whose writings had posed and disseminated a monumental challenge to the Eurocentric version of African history, is not.

Further, the sole reference to Rodney is not in his capacity as a historian but as an organizer of the Sixth Pan African Congress. And it is hardly a positive reference. Reading between the lines, we gather that by inciting 'an unfortunate fight over ideologies,' Rodney was partly responsible for the paucity of accomplishments at this historic gathering (pp 304-5).

Asante provides a partial and distorted version of what transpired at the Congress. With no explication of the contentious issues, Rodney comes out as a pesky Marxist who, by raising tangential matters like the international class struggle, prevented well-meaning African patriots from uniting based on a common agenda. Asante, yet, is silent about the tendency of many African scholars of that era to side with the West in the sharp divide created by the Cold War. He does not say that Rodney's critique was directed at scholars like Ali Mazrui who stood, at that time, in the way of the flowering of a nonaligned, independent, progressive African scholarship in history and the social sciences. Rodney held that to unite based on tenets that did not challenge neo-colonialism would harm the people of Africa. That was the crucial lesson he strove to inculcate at the Congress, and it remains as relevant today as it was then.

Asante (2007), for its part, aims to counter Eurocentrism by providing thematic centrality to the complex historic experience of Africa, and by stressing the ignored notion of African agency.

Declarations are one thing, and contents, quite another. Despite isolated mentions of relevant facts, the book fails to give a modicum of a picture of the extensive interventions – political, military, economic and cultural — by the US, UK and France in post-colonial Africa. These actions decisively reduced the ability of Africa to stand on its own feet. There is only a limited coverage of the numerous grassroots struggles mounted by students, peasants, workers, and small shopkeepers to counter internal and neo-colonial injustice. The idea of giving agency to African people in this book is essentially a narration of the deeds of the elites. The history of Tanzania, thus, is reduced mainly to the actions of one person. Overall, the book focuses on culture and politics but is weak and inconsistent on economic aspects, internal and external.

The last chapter appears promising at the outset. Entitled 'Towards a United States of Africa without compromise', it deals with political unity, economic development, health, and other issues. The highlight is on the role played by Africa's current leaders in achieving the desirable goals. Libya's Muammar Gaddafi is praised for his unifying agenda. African intellectuals and Africans in diaspora are posited as the central players in this effort. The former group includes cultural and political patriots and a few prominent Marxists. We encounter radical words like imperialism, continental marginalization, external agenda, dependency, economic self-reliance, etc., sprinkled here and there. And the book ends with a proposed preamble for the constitution of the United States of Africa that any well-meaning African would take to heart.

Yet, it is hollow talk. The current African reality is not frankly displayed. That virtually all of the present day leaders of Africa, both the named and unnamed, have surrendered the economic resources and even setting the priorities for their nations to multinational firms, external 'donors' and short-sighted, avaricious local tycoons; that they have turned their nations into places of stupendous inequality and political chicanery, that they have overseen the entrenchment of intellectual and cultural narrow mindedness and dependency, that they have created an atmosphere of grotesque donor-worship and widespread, unbridled corruption; such harsh truths are glossed over in this book. Agency is a dance among the esteemed elites; the common person is but a spectator.

In contrast, Rodney, with his bold, uncompromising and consistent stand against all entities blocking Africa's right to self-determination on social, economic, and political fronts, remains head and shoulder above Asante (2007) as the champion of genuine African agency.

Asante's book was written to uncover and elucidate the set of thematic principles governing African history. Yet, by the time you reach the last page, you scratch your head and wonder what they actually are and what their rationale is. The thing you can say is that whatever they are, they are quite compatible with the neo-liberal economic agenda and hollow democracy championed by the Western nations.

## COLLINS AND BURNS (2007)

*HEUA* is listed in two chapter-wise Further Readings, and *HUGC* is listed in one. A quote from Rodney explains the nature of the colonial labor and cash crop policies (pp 314-5).

The basis thesis of the chapter, headed the Colonial Legacy, reflects the thesis of *HEUA*: 'European pressure distorted African economic growth and led to the underdevelopment of the continent.' Furthermore, this thesis is also explicitly debated over two pages (311-2). Among the books under review, this book gives the fairest acknowledgement to Rodney and has the most accurate assessment of his impact on African history.

The reason these authors give for regarding *HEUA* as a highly important work is particularly striking, as it is none other than the abject failure of the development policies adopted across Africa after Independence. They recognize the persistence of the features of underdevelopment as defined by Rodney as the main explanation for those failures. They also summarize in a reasonable manner Rodney's systemic arguments against the stand of the scholars who claim that colonialism was of some benefit to Africa as well. His relevance to modern day political activism in and about Africa is also pointed out.

In accordance with the approach of *HEUA*, Collins and Burns (2007) pay due attention to economic factors, illustrate their distortive impact, and connect economic issues with the socio-political trends in the African nations. At several places, the role of Western imperialism in blocking progress in Africa is highlighted.

Nonetheless, the book is afflicted with a grave anomaly. The first four chapters of Part IV reflect the above delineated Rodney-oriented spirit. The fifth chapter, the final chapter, however, makes a total turnaround, both in substance and method.

Once the book reaches the era of neo-liberal globalization, the notions of dependency and imperialism are cast aside. The explanatory factors and possible solutions to Africa's predicament come to reflect the spirit of neo-liberalism. The established imperialists are mysteriously reborn as democratically oriented, 'less ideologically driven donors' concerned with poverty reduction, good governance, beneficial market driven policies and the like (p 383). Without explanation or supportive facts, Rodney's basic thesis is turned up-side down.

At one point, Collins and Burns (2007) show discomfort with the style of *HEUA*, calling it 'polemical' and 'inflammatory' but concede that it did raise the popularity of the book. Despite the initial similarities with Rodney's approach, this book does not declare its own framework in a clear fashion at any point. Rodney's systemic, long-term framework is not embraced explicitly. Such critical shortcomings permit the authors not only to make an unexpected flip-flop at the end but also to change their tune into a contrarily emotive one. Thus, they represent 'Mali under Modibo Keita.... [as] an economic satellite of the East European countries' (p 362). This is but a half-truth. Yet, it is taken, without good evidence, as an uncontroversial statement. But, to say, in the style and spirit of Rodney, that Congo under Mobutu and Liberia under Tubman were US neo-colonies, would be using emotive terms, engaging in conspiracy theories, or promoting communist propaganda.

It is a time honored tradition to regard a statement, however polemical or inflammatory, to be objective and of scholarly expression provided it is in line with the mainstream vision of society.

## FREUND (1998)

This book, the only of the eight books to explicitly and almost consistently adopt a Marxist approach to historical analysis, has two entries for Rodney in the Index. The Annotated Bibliography, presented in a chapter by chapter manner, lists papers of Rodney published in scholarly journals. But *HUGC* does not appear in there.

Freund (1998), though, casts Walter Rodney in an entirely different light. According to him, Rodney was not a Marxist. This is mainly because for him the notion of dependency championed by Rodney is not a Marxist but a vague, nationalistic idea. It promotes a catch-all, fixed view that underplays the dynamism of capitalism noted by Marx, avoids internal class analysis, marginalizes the variations in the economic and social patterns and class contradictions, and so on. Due to such flaws, Freund finds the development of underdevelopment theory not to have a sound basis and not Marxist in character (p 11).

In essence thereby, he deems Rodney but a radical nationalist. To quote him in full:

> In 1972, the Guyanese Walter Rodney, himself one of the most critical and far-ranging of Africanists, published How Europe Underdeveloped Africa. Although, as the title indicates, Rodney's polemic was continental (and by implication, radical), and he betrayed much of the influence of the earlier idealist and romantic Afro-American nationalist understanding of Africa, his book represented a powerful and effective break with the positivism of the Africanists (p 10).

Radical yes; Marxist, surely not. Rodney's decisive influence on African historiography in terms of the consideration of economic factors and on adopting a long-term, systemic framework is not acknowledged either. For his part, Freund (1998) locates his calling within Basil Davidson's project to 'present the essential unity of Africa with the people of the rest of the world' but 'in a materialist context' (p 13).

Freund (1998) thereupon brings to the fore a far-ranging body of credible work ignored by almost all historians of today to construct a remarkably dynamic picture of Africa, rooted in class and economic analysis, over the recent two-hundred-year period. Yet, it is interesting to note that his evidence in large measure lends support to the thesis that imperial dependency, while changing in form, constituted a key feature of that historic process. Rather than being mutually exclusive entities, external economic relations and internal class contradictions affect each other in a complementary or contentious, namely dialectical, manner at varied historic junctures.

Freund's criticism of Rodney is off the mark. First, *HUGC*, Rodney's doctoral thesis derived book, reveals his awareness of the importance of internal social stratification. He traces the complex evolution of the main communities of Upper Guinea Coast, depicts their social, cultural, political and economic features in a lively, integrated manner, elucidates in a colorful style their interactions with the initial bands of European traders, and so on. Overall, we are regaled with a vibrant historic tapestry of social change that takes both internal and external forces and social relations into account.

Second, Freund (1998) does not recognize a key difference between *HUGC* and *HEUA*. Even as the latter has a wider continental scope, its thematic scope, as specified by the title, is a limited one. While *HUGC* is a general history of a specific region, *HEUA* is not a general history of Africa. It is more akin to an economic history of Africa.

Yet, despite that difference in focus, *HEUA* does not, as noted earlier, ignore pertinent societal analysis. It does not invoke the development of underdevelopment model in a mechanistic fashion. Where relevant, he employs an integrated analysis in which the structures of economic and political domination generated by external forces interacted with local class formation to change the reality on the ground. That emerges, for example, in his description of colonial education. Rodney observes that while that the education system was established to serve the needs of colonial administration and economy, over time, it also produced the grave-diggers of colonial rule. It created a social stratum that rose above the masses, yet, that stratum later mobilized the masses first to reform and then to eliminate colonial rule. While specific aspects of Rodney's analysis of dependency and class relations can be improved, expanded or corrected in terms what is known now, his general approach stands securely in place. As noted in the last chapter, Rodney pays adequate attention to internal and external social and class relations in *HEUA* but, for the sake of retaining focus, does not give sufficient coverage to internal and external social and class struggles. Freund does not seem to have read the book well.

The issue of the character of social divisions produced by imperial domination has divided the Marxist community. Is there a ruling class within such nations? High economic dependency coexists with a comprador, subservient local ruling entity while loosening of such bonds denotes the rise of a more nationalistic, autonomous group of capitalists at the helm of the local state. However, as the post-colonial nations in Africa and Asia demonstrate, it is not a mutually exclusive situation; elements of both are always present, though one may dominate over the other as the form and nature of external domination changes. The presence of intermediary economic classes (European settlers, Asian or Lebanese merchants) with non-indigenous roots, at least at the outset, produces more complex relationships in the colonial as well as post-colonial times. In Tanzania, for example, the first three decades of Independence within a state-capitalist, nominally socialist formation, the local ruling class was a nationalistic entity and stood in contradiction with the mainly Asian commercial bourgeoisie. After the onset of full scale neo-liberalism in the 1990s, a comprador, multi-ethnic class connected to state institutions and increasingly subservient to US imperialism, has assumed the reins of power. While growth in several areas of the economy is evident, the bonds of dependency together with internal inequalities and social misery have intensified too.

After posing the question about the existence of ruling classes in Africa, Freund (1998) declares they have a national bourgeoisie character and they should not be seen as undifferentiated groups of compradors.

> [Countries] such as Kenya ought to be seen primarily as developing capitalist states with the indigenous ruling class, its foreign allies notwithstanding, in fundamental contradiction to the masses rather than an undifferentiated 'neo-colonialism' or 'imperialism' represented locally by a thin stratum of agents or stooges (p 212).

By posing the question simplistically, Freund (1998) sets up a 'strawman' so as to strike it down with ease. His declared affinity to Tanzania notwithstanding, he fails to refer to the rich, extended debate on this and related issues at the University of Dar es Salaam during the 1970s. Rodney was a key participant in the debates. His stand, evolving over time, was nuanced, not simplistic. See Rodney (1972b;1973;1980a), Shivji (2012), and related papers in the student Marxist journal *Cheche* that was renamed after 1970 as *MajiMaji*.

Like any science, Marxism is a dynamic discipline. Issues of contention arise now and then. Varied views on the ideas of dependency and ruling class form a part of the Marxist tradition. By dismissing those with whom he disagrees, Freund (1998) exhibits unwarranted intellectual hubris. And his stand has many holes too. For, by him, Mathieu Kerekou was a 'Marxist dictator' (p 262) but Rodney was not a Marxist.

Freund's model of the reality is binary one: either class relations or economic structures; either extraction of surplus value or unequal exchange; either total dependency or full autonomy; with no interplay between the two poles, and no room for dynamic evolution as a result of that interplay. Eventually, his one-sided stand and the concomitant neglect of external forces and dependency become his undoing. We find that the closer we are to the present era, the more diffuse and un-Marxist his class and economic analyses become, and the closer his views approach the dominant neoliberal ideology.

Thereby, the grotesque role played by the US in undermining economic progress and human rights in Africa after 1960 is minimally exposed. The clearly deleterious effects of liberalization, privatization and foreign investments are barely shown. Instead, he resorts to the hollow rhetoric of democracy and freedom to explain the socio-political events. Thus, we find declarations like:

> If the American embassy in Nairobi had become the linchpin in the drive for democratisation in Kenya, its willingness to endorse the re-election of Moi in 1992 marked the end of the drive (p 262).

Since when can an arrogant imperial power known for brutal, unilateral invasions, fomenting death squad regimes, military dictatorships and, at best, demonstration democracies, ever be deemed a promoter of democracy? What of the Marxist notions of state power and bourgeois democracy? To firmly support a dictator at one time and reject him at another, to promote 'democracy' at one point in time, and reject it soon afterwards — such contradictory actions have for long characterized the US policy across the globe (Epstein 2015).

In the final pages of this book we find a mixture of potent criticism of aspects of neoliberal globalization as well as capitulation to its recipes. This occurs in relation to matters like liberalization, privatization, NGOs led development, the role of World Bank and IMF, US interventions in Africa, and many more. Mal-developments in education and health are not well addressed.

With Freund's positing an indigenous ruling class, we expect he would bring to the fore the multitude of working class, student, professional struggles and peasant uprisings that have occurred across Africa in the recent years. He would also address the internal divisions and massive destabilization in these societies in terms of class analysis. He would highlight the wholesale looting of public coffers by the local oligarchs and corrupt political strata and the emergence of multi-millionaire dominated electoral processes. We expect an explication of the trends in modern African economies through the Marxist notions of accumulation and surplus value extraction.

He does no such thing. Apparently envisioning the blooming of a vibrant and democratic society with the help of the international donors, he casts aside his Marxist method, and seeks the saving grace for Africa in the realms of culture, sports and related activities.

> In fact, out of hard times, creativity and originality are also being born, and Africa's integration with, and influence on, our contemporary world deepens (p 267).

Afrocentric scholars reject Rodney because of his Marxism, an ideology of foreign origin. The Marxist disavows him for his (Afrocentric) black nationalism Yet, ultimately, the Marxist holds hands with staunch anti-Marxist Afrocentric historians to dance for the imperial neoliberals and the local bourgeoisie. On the other hand, Rodney, castigated by them as one who ignored local struggles and the common people, sacrifices his life in a rough, down to earth struggle against an alliance of the local and imperial bourgeois classes in his homeland. Yet, this duality appears as a paradox only if one views theory and praxis as disjoint activities.

## ILIFFE (2007)

The index of this widely used text by an eminent Cambridge historian who once taught at the University of Dar es Salaam has no entry related to Rodney. It does quote *HEUA* to describe the colonial taxation policy (p 205 and p 324) but *HEUA* is not listed in any of its extensive lists of material for further reading.

Iliffe demarcates three post-1950s strand of African historiography: the anti-colonial/nation-building strand, the economic/underdevelopment strand and the recent environmental/social issues focused strand. His book, he declares, integrates important features of all the three strands, and pays particular attention to demographic issues. It is noteworthy that while Marxist historians earn the pejorative label 'disillusioned,' those of his camp of conventional historians are depicted in a neutral fashion. The historians who don the Afrocentric perspective are not recognized as a noteworthy group.

The influence of *HEUA* on African history has become so ingrained that even a traditionalist like Iliffe cannot evade it. Like other conventional historians now, his book too pays reasonable attention, at least up to the end of the colonial period, to economic issues, and does it in a somewhat decent manner. Other than that, he consistently ignores the insights of the underdevelopment strand. Rodney, its principal theorist, is barely heeded. Overall, one can say Iliffe's text is based on a framework that is plainly opposed to Rodney's. This is most evident in his account of the post-colonial era.

Here are a few points in that respect: Terms such as underdevelopment, imperialism, dependency and neo-colonialism do not grace the index but neo-liberal concepts like structural adjustment, poverty reduction and New Economic Policy for African Development (NEPAD) do. While the term underdevelopment appears in two places in the text, no distinction is made between economic growth and economic development. The World Bank is brought in at a couple of places in connection with the structural adjustment policies of the 1980s but the discussion lacks insight or depth. That it was the World

Bank policies in Africa since Independence that contributed to their high indebtedness and economic travails of that decade is ignored.

The most striking demonstration of the pro-imperial, neo-liberal bias of Iliffe (2007) is the deletion from African history of the plethora events and outcomes that put the West in a negative light, especially in the post-colonial era. The USA, a nation that played a decisive but detrimental role in African affairs, is absent from the Index and practically absent in the text as well.

More can be said, but what has been stated suffices to illustrate the existence of a camouflaged bias against ideas like class and economic analysis, dependency and neo-colonialism in this text. This not only casts doubt on Iliffe's initial assertion of using insights from all three strands, but because he fails to provide any justification for ignoring such ideas, his stand cannot be deemed a scholarly one. Is it that prominent historians at prestigious institutions lack the conceptual wherewithal to confront Rodney head on? Moreover, the extensive list of political-economy related references for African in Freund (1998) and which are ignored by Iliffe (2007) provides a good indication of the extent of bias of omission (against leftist works, even those based on in-depth research) present in Iliffe (2007) and similar texts.

And by the time the reader reaches the last page of this venerated text, he or she will not have a picture of how the author has selected the tenets from the three strands of African historiography to formulate his own integrated framework of historic analysis. The grandiose declaration at the outset remains just that – a declaration without substance.

John Iliffe was housed in the same department at the University of Dar es Salaam as Walter Rodney. They were contemporaries for several years. And Iliffe was not a scholar who confined himself libraries and archives. Among radical students, he had the reputation of a staunchly anti-Marxist academic. His research seminars were characterized by hot exchanges with the leftist students.

Persistent curricular reform pursued by progressive academics like Lionel Cliffe, Sol Piciotto, Walter Rodney, John Saul, Tamas Szentes and others over a five-year period resulted in an influential pedagogic innovation at the university. This was in the form of an interdisciplinary course, Development Studies, that was taught from a political economy perspective. Undergraduate students in all the departments were required to take it or an equivalent course. The main aim of the course was to impart a well-documented overall perspective on the nation and the world, past, present and prospective futures, to all students, be they in medicine, physics, engineering, law or another field. It was not meant to supplant specialized disciplines like history, sociology or economics but complement them. This pioneering course was later emulated by universities in Africa and beyond.

Yet the process of establishing and sustaining it was an uphill battle. It was stridently opposed by specialty oriented conservative academics, local and foreign. Even as it was designed to follow required standards and was taught eminent scholars, they claimed that it would dilute the standards. One person in the forefront of this ideologically driven opposition was John Iliffe. In 1970, a group of seven reactionary academics signed a petition to the university authorities whose recommendations included abolishing the Department of Development Studies and effectively nullifying the novel aspects of the course. The only non-Tanzanian signatory was John Iliffe. The petition was strongly condemned in a statement issued by progressive students, and fortunately, was not adopted by the university senate.

Bias during colonial rule was clear and explicit. In the neo-colonial and neo-liberal times, it is subtle and covert. Ideological anchoring towards the *status quo* can confound the conceptual horizons of a scholar as effectively as it does that of a person in the street.

## LAUMANN (2012)

This, the slimmest of the eight texts under review, lists Rodney twice in the index. The introduction declares *HEUA* a 'classic [Marxist] work' and 'a popular and powerful survey' that was 'extremely influential' in its time. Laumann credits it with challenging the 'traditional interpretations of colonialism' and pointing 'the way to new areas of study for historians' (p xvi). Despite this laudatory start, in the penultimate paragraph of his book, Rodney is branded essentially as a scholar with a lop-sided, rigid outlook. Laumann proceeds to pitch his tent with the balance-sheet (good-versus-bad) based, allegedly nuanced and objective, approach to colonial history. This approach has risen in popularity among Africa oriented scholars of these post-socialist times (p 82).

Laumann's eventual capitulation comes as a surprise. For, despite its brevity, his book packs a good Marxist oriented punch, and is replete with concepts Rodney popularized. Instead of equating imperialism with colonialism, he defines it as 'the process of one group of people extending its economic, political, or social power over other peoples' (p xi). Opening the first chapter — on economics — with the Leninist definition of imperialism, Laumann categorically states that the 'central assumption' of the chapter is that 'economic motives and factors were the key driving forces for the European conquest of Africa' (p 1). Marxist notions like comprador class, merchant class, and neo-colonialism appear in the book as well.

The final chapter on the modern era focuses on economics, and draws, *à la* Rodney, upon the Marxian notion of neo-colonialism. Quotes from African scholars elaborate its deleterious effects. Yet, just at the end, rather than call for deeper study of neo-colonialism and its social effects, Laumann, just like others, lands squarely in the lap of neo-liberalism.

As before, the central flaw is that he does not explicitly posit a coherent, interdisciplinary framework for historic analysis. Despite mentioning the various approaches to African history at the outset, his own approach is nowhere specified with any degree of clarity. The topic at hand affects how he visualizes history; consequently, his framework seems to vary from chapter to chapter. That fluidity enables him to easily make a total about face at the end. The sole rationale for that reversal is an out-of-context quote from *HEUA* that, taken on its own, makes Rodney look like a purely emotive historian.

An ultimate declaration of preference for the good-versus-bad approach makes his book politically more palatable. It avoids vexing queries from established historians. One does not then need to inquire: if the basic factors underlying colonial rule were economic, and since those economic objectives were pursued in a consistently ruthless manner, could not it be that all this talk about democracy, good governance and partnership in development from the West is a mask for an equally nefarious neo-colonialism? His approach permits the imperialists to be reborn as altruistic benefactors who make mistakes but whose intent is noble. The principal responsibility for the daunting problems besieging Africa is shifted exclusively onto its corrupt rulers. This smooth transition from Marxism-Leninism to rationalization of neo-liberalism is a good indicator of the convoluted state of progressive African historiography today.

## READER (1999)

In this 800-page volume from a seasoned British journalist, both *HEUA* and *HUGC* are listed in the references, though Rodney does not appear in the Index. *HEUA* appears thrice in the text notes; once in relation to existence of class distinctions in pre-colonial Africa (p 297) and twice in connection with education and the formation of a privileged elite during the colonial era, and its consequences (p 627).

Simultaneously a popular and an academic work, it aims to rectify the portrayal of a 'woefully misunderstood and misused' continent (p x) as it decries 'the whiff of prejudice ... detectable in some quarters even at the end of the twentieth century' (p 238). Overall, the book does a fairly satisfactory job, presenting an adequate picture of Africa at least into the early colonial period. It is also strong in presenting details about the economy and economic relations until that era, a reflection of the long-term influence of Rodney and his fellow Marxists.

In several places, Reader (1999) adopts a thunderous anti-Western tone in a Rodney like spirit. For example, the revealing chapter entitled 'Harnessed to Europe' ends:

> Were it not for the importunities of Europe, Africa might have enlarged upon its indigenous talents and found an independent route to the present one that was inspired by resolution from within rather than examples from outside. The moment passed, however, during the fifteenth century and cannot be retrieved. Since then the history of Africa has been the story of an ancient continent and its inhabitants trying to accommodate the concerns of modern humans whose ancestors left the cradle-land 100,000 years ago (see Chapter 10), and who came back 500 years ago, behaving as if they owned the place (p 368).

Nonetheless, the coverage of Africa from the 1950s onwards is a major disappointment. The presentation is lop-sided, replete with not just whiffs but wholesale prejudices of mainstream Western journalism on Africa. Significant matters about the economy are ignored or distorted. The interdisciplinary perspective is ditched in its entirety. As the multiplicity of problems – political instability, military coups, authoritarianism, internal strife, etc. – are highlighted, the crucial role played by the US and other Western powers in blocking economic progress, rule of law, and real democracy across Africa is swept under the rug. It is forgotten that these powers continue to behave, to this day, as if they own the place. Instead, the terminology and tone of benevolent neo-liberalism are employed to diagnose existing problems and point to a better future for Africa.

Once again, the absence of an explicit, consistent framework for historical analysis in the book makes such a flip-flop not a surprise.

## REID (2012)

This is the only book that, among all under review, has no reference to Rodney or his work in any shape or form. After critiquing the derogatory colonial works on African history, Reid attends to the corrective nationalistic approach that bloomed after Independence. In the Introduction, he says that the University of Dar es Salaam was a key center in that endeavor. Yet his Further Reading list contains only one of the many stellar works produced at that university. Instead, the list is dominated by the culturally oriented Afrocentric titles. Major non-Marxist historians are also set side.

The contents of this book, though, are at variance with these omissions. The author starts with the issue of formation of multi-faceted identities and lays out the themes of the book. Among them are economic affairs and economic domination by the West. And this is how economic issues are dealt with at numerous places. The Index of this book has more entries relating development and underdevelopment than any of the other books under review. Further, the usage of these ideas is consistent with *HEUA*. There is reasonable coverage of labor related issues, and terms like neo-colonialism and Western neo-imperialism are employed occasionally.

Having said that, Reid's work lacks a consistently deployed, coherent analytic framework. Possibly, it is the most deficient among the books under review in that respect. Superficial and skewed discussions of health and education in Africa are oddly followed by a perceptive take on the difference between economic growth and economic development. Many critical comments on the role of the US in Africa are given, yet the role played by President Bill Clinton in Africa is narrated in a decidedly selective, biased and misleading style.

Explicitly and implicitly, different sections of the book portray Rodney's perspective in different lights, favorable and unfavorable. The ideas he championed and those he staunchly opposed exist in a harmonious manner in these pages.

## SHILLINGTON (2012)

The two entries for Rodney in the Index refer to *HEUA* at a place in the text where it is called a 'highly influential' work. The Africanist works by Diop (1974) and Asante (2007) earn the label 'influential' yet 'controversial.' Shillington states in the Introduction that his exposition draws upon elements of the Africanist approach and the Marxist approach.

To cap his presentation, Shillington gives a list of 231 sources for further reading. It covers almost the totality of all the literature cited in the book, and is divided according to categories like general history, methodology, specific themes, periods and regions.

Diop (1974), Asante (2007) and another Afrocentric book appear in this list under works of methodology or influential works that challenged the Eurocentric vision. Rodney, surprisingly, is not listed in these sections or anywhere else. Despite the high praise given at the outset, a full citation for *HEUA* does not appear anywhere in Shillington (2012).

Yet the impact of *HEUA* is evident throughout his book. As with many present-day historians of Africa, Shillington's exposition of pre-European contact history integrates the dimensions of environment, economy, social stratification, political order and culture in a manner that comes close to a Marxist approach. Economic and environmental factors are accorded a major role in social dynamics. Shillington goes further than many to retain that approach well into the slave trade, colonial and post-colonial eras. The primary motivation for colonial rule, for example, is stated as economic – resources and markets. His characterization of colonial education is in Rodney-like terms:

> Basically, colonial governments were only interested in training a small elite to fill the lower rungs of the administrative service. They saw mass education as a danger to be avoided (pp 372-3).

Particularly, Shillington credits Rodney for bringing the crucial issue of adverse terms of trade to the forefront (p 447, yet missed in the Index). Many details of continued deleterious Western economic interventions in post-Independent Africa are noted. The term 'neo-colonialism' appears in several places, and the so-called globalization is aptly portrayed as neo-colonialism in new clothes (p 451).

Yet, with Shillington as well, the closer one comes to the present day, the more eclectic the approach. The familiar virus of proximity corrodes his critical stance. The varied dimensions of society are no longer as coherently linked. The final four chapters that come up to the 2010s contain valid, critical observations on external economic interference and domination. But matters of politics and society appear in a form that gives the impression of purely localized strife and problems.

For Shillington, bold declarations like globalization is a new form of neo-colonialism are fluid declarations. They do not inform his approach in a consistent manner. Unlike Rodney, he does not posit imperialism as a global economic system that continues to generate the structures of dependency and domination in distinctive and dynamic forms. He fails to explain the phenomenon of underdevelopment and does not make the crucial distinction between economic growth and economic development. The perfidious role played by the US in post-colonial Africa is only partly brought up. Much more is hidden from view. In the spirit of Western neo-liberal ideology, China is disparaged for being oblivious to democratic progress in Africa, whilst the West is depicted as the promoter of freedom and good governance.

## CONCLUSION

Western presence in Africa over a five-hundred-year period created an underdeveloped continent while the transfer of wealth from Africa helped the rise of a developed West. This well documented message of *HEUA* made the historians of Africa pay attention to the Marxist method and many universities used it as a textbook for African studies courses.

Today, the presence of *HEUA* in the classroom has diminished greatly. Students now encounter Rodney and *HEUA* mainly from other books. My survey of eight prominent works used in teaching African history leads to the following conclusions about how the students encounter Rodney and his principal work:

1. The influence of the Marxist approach to African history, of which the *HEUA* was the supreme work, undeniably persists to this day. Issues about the economy, the deleterious impact of the economic relations with the West and the strong effects of economic factors on social and political change, issues that were controversial in the sixties, have now become acceptable and are generally present in the texts being used teach African history.
2. Yet, such books generally lack a coherent and explicitly formulated framework for historical analysis and rarely delineate the primary explanatory factors. The framework and factors often change from chapter to chapter. Obscurity often overpowers illumination.
3. The economic perspective students encounter in such books will not be systematic or consistent. The closer one gets to the present era, the firmer will the alignment with the dominant neo-liberal mode of thought to be.
4. Despite the paradigm shifting contribution of the Marxist school to the study of African history, students will rarely find a fair depiction or acknowledgement of that contribution. Rodney, the principal spokesman of that school, is accorded similar treatment.
5. If any direct references to Rodney or *HEUA* are made, they will tend to be ambivalent or distorted. He or his book may be praised at the start but then assiduously ignored or grossly misrepresented in the later pages. Some books portray him as an emotive activist, with a rigid approach to African history.
6. Such verdicts on Rodney or his ideas will not derive from a detailed, scholarly analysis. Often, they will be based on taking one or two sentences from *HEUA* out of context to make him appear the opposite of what he stood for. Such unfounded verdicts on Rodney come from historians of all variety, Afrocentric, nationalistic, Marxist, environmentally-oriented, post-colonial historians, or adherents of other styles of history.

Admittedly, these conclusions derive from a limited sample of books that was selected in a subjective fashion. However, because the books span a broad spectrum of approaches to African history, I conjecture that they will hold up in a wider survey as well.

The depth of the bias against a first-rate historian who was at the same time a revolutionary activist within the present day academic community is loud and clear. That he effectively challenged their prejudices and injected activism into the conservative, staid environments of university history departments does not sit well with establishment historians. They remain captive to the stultified, flawed but professionally and politically palatable ideas of neo-liberalism. Whatever their professed approach to history, they ultimately succumb to the pro-Western lore of free markets, liberalization, entrepreneurship, donor assistance, and democracy as the sole way for Africa to progress. Despite their claims of objectivity, these historians have no qualms in setting aside the volumes of evidence that points to the opposite conclusion.

The principal lesson from this survey is that for a student seeking to learn about Rodney and his ideas, there is no shortcut. He or she has to read *HEUA*. The continued significance of its ideas for the analysis and understanding of the current state of African nations and their potential future trajectories, make it strongly advisable for him or her to seriously study this book.

Furthermore, combining that with reading Rodney's *History of the Upper Guinea Coast, 1540 to 1800* will produce a greater appreciation of his historical acumen. This book is a rich, multi-faceted depiction of the complexities – in terms of culture, customs, economy, politics, social stratification, ruling institutions, relations between local ethnic groupings and interactions with traders, visitors and colonizers from Europe – in a period from around the initial European contact to before the onset of full European incursion into a particular region of Africa. It puts to rest charges against Rodney that he only dealt with external factors, that he had a rigid, deterministic framework, that he did not consider internal class factors, that he denied agency to the people of Africa, etc.

Reading the two books together makes it clear that the negative charges placed against Rodney and *HEUA* stem in large measure from political bias and superficial perusal rather than from scholarly, historiographical investigations.

CHAPTER 8

## CONTEMPORARY RELEVANCE

*H*EUA's prognostications for post-Independence Africa have turned out to be stunningly accurate. Independent African nations, even those that had declared themselves Marxist, at best took a few baby steps to disengage from the structural economic shackles set up in the colonial era. Other than getting some assistance from socialist countries, they stuck to the economic prescriptions handed out by the IMF and the World Bank. As the new ruling groups devoted themselves to lining their pockets and consolidating their hold on state power, the old structures of dependency were altered only in minor, quantitative ways. A decade of modest growth was followed by stagnation, eroding social services and high levels of indebtedness. This gave the imperial financial institutions the power to impose policies even more harmful to the wellbeing of the ordinary people. Five decades on, Africa remains an exploited frontier of the global capitalist system. Its resources, land, and labor still serve external economies and multinational firms while it remains industrially backward and imports basic agricultural and other necessities. The few industries set up in the early days of Independence have been eviscerated in the latest onslaught of global capitalism (Burgis 2015; Deardon 2015; Editor 2015; McCauley 2015).

Economic growth in many nations has been high of recent. For the most part, it has been driven by foreign dominated oil, gas, mining and tourism sectors. But it is a transient phenomenon: a few years of boom invariably lead to a prolonged bust. And, as Rodney taught us, growth and development are distinct entities.

The presence of the former is seen in the luxurious, high rise dwellings, casinos and beach resorts for the expatriates and the local elite while the lack of latter is manifested in persistent malnutrition in rural areas and schools for which pencils and pens have to be imported, and where the ratio of students to teacher exceeds 200 to one, students sit on the ground, and have no books. Seven years of such education fails to enable many to read, write, or multiply even at a minimal level (Hickel 2014).

Rodney's emphasis on basic economic issues, on tackling dependency, on standing on one's own feet is of more than historic interest; it is vital to the construction of policies of benefit to the broad masses of Africa. His systemic mode of analysis is indispensable for uncovering the nature of the impact of pro-corporate globalization on Africa. Many micro level studies to date have yielded a mountain of evidence of the deleterious nature of this impact; but they have yet to be interconnected within the context of a social system.

That deficiency stems from the prevailing tendency to analyze the African past and present in fragmented, biased ways which mask the facts and essence of neo-colonial domination. In his time, Rodney stridently tackled the political scientists, historians, development theorists and sociologists, from Africa and beyond, who, while donning the mantle of African patriotism, adopted such a stand. His sharp debates with Ali Mazrui, a prominent doyen of that school, are the stuff of legend. Yet, over the years, Mazrui, to his credit, became more critical towards Western interference in Africa. But he retained his cultural-nationalistic viewpoint to his last day. Noting economic matters and integrating them into his analysis was a virtual taboo for him.

In our neoliberal times, this Mazrui type of world view dominates the work of Africa oriented scholars, local and foreign. The terminology has changed but the retrogressive essence persists. The phenomenon affects not just the scholars who have recently come of age. Many astute academics of yesterday who had adopted the leftist, holistic conceptual framework have, in the changed political climate, shed their radical garb and migrated towards the safer shores of effusive cultural, post-colonial, identity-based forms of analyses that side line the economic dimension of globalization and the continued systematic grip of imperialism on Africa. Not to do so risks the loss of funding for your work.

## AN INSTRUCTIVE EXAMPLE

The Ugandan political scientist Mahmood Mamdani is a case in point. An erstwhile Marxist and colleague of Rodney at the University of Dar es Salaam, he authored well regarded leftist books like *Politics and Class Formation in Uganda* and *Imperialism and Fascism in Uganda* in that era (Mamdani 1976;1984).

To this day, he remains a prolific, respected, award winning writer on African issues. Yet, while a few of his writings still display a critical stand on the Western role in global affairs (Mamdani 2005), his conceptual horizon has shifted in a fundamental way. Economic issues and ideas like underdevelopment, imperialism, neo-colonialism, neo-liberalism and class analysis are no longer germane to his analytic method. Instead, he operates on the legal, political, and cultural planes with identity group, ethnicity, religion, race, tribe, and nation as his basic units of analysis. His focus is on politics, law, administration and conflict resolution, with class and anti-imperialist struggles deleted from the picture. Insightful and well researched as his analysis is, it is incomplete and biased as it avoids the underlying reality and economic trends that constitutes the long-term foundation for the problems he examines. That decades of material plight, ill health, hunger, empty promises, and political repression foment popular moods that lead to proliferation of divisive, hateful, regressive, religious and ethnic outlooks is secondary in his framework. And that such realities are in no small way the outcome of five decades of economic prescriptions and measures emanating from, and harshly enforced by, the West and the international financial institutions is secondary to him. The role of Western military intervention in initiating the slide into chaos and mayhem is marginalized. It is then no surprise that he can pontificate on the recent convulsions in Egypt without a word on the role of the US in the process. For him, it is just a question of Africans getting their act together and learning the ABC's of peaceful, democratic co-existence (Mamdani 2008a; 2008b; 2011).

Mamdani's recent monograph, *Define and Rule: Native as Political Identity*, well encapsulates his current conceptual framework for social and historical analysis (Mamdani 2012). Its aim is to unravel the notion of identity in the colonial and post-colonial African contexts.

The anti-colonial rebellions of the 19th century in India and elsewhere form his stage of departure. Revealing the unstable nature of direct colonial rule, they presaged a new mode administering the colonies. With a detailed explication of the views of politically influential scholars like Henry Maine, he depicts the theory and practice of indirect colonial rule. A host of concrete case-studies from Asia and Africa are given. He then offers us the critical insights of African historians like Yusuf Bala Usman on indirect rule and its consequences. The book reaches its climax with an extended description of the process of dismantling the vestiges of indirect rule and creation of a unified nation-state in Tanzania under Julius K Nyerere. That process, according to him, epitomizes the possibility of peacefully establishing a modern state in Africa that is based on equal legal and political rights and a unitary administrative framework for all citizens.

Indirect rule, Mamdani tells us, was predicated upon positing two primary social groups in the society: natives and settlers, each governed by distinct administrative structures and laws. The natives were categorized into tribes and the non-natives (settlers) into races. A key, stated aim was to respect and protect the culture and customs of the natives from external intrusion while placing the settlers under a European style of governance.

Theory was one thing, practice quite another. As Mamdani demonstrates, this strategy of divide and rule did not stand on traditional or existing social groupings. Rather, it rested on policies that defined and cemented artificial identities. (All page numbers in this section refer to Mamdani (2012)).

> The British actively defined and shaped community identities (p 29).

> The architects of indirect rule had vast ambitions: to remake subjectivities so as to realign its bearers. This was no longer just divide and rule. It was define and rule (p 42).

Yet, artificial as they were, these identities became ingrained into the socio-political landscape. The take-home message is that the persistence and intensification of colonially derived identities — based on race and tribe — lie at the root of the instability and strife that plagues African nations today. And further, that the path to social harmony lies in pursuing, in the spirit of Julius Nyerere of Tanzania, cohesive, conciliatory and peaceful strategies that will promote a unified sense national identity.

Sensible and noble as it sounds, Mamdani's case has fundamental flaws. Taking him on his own terms, we see that simply focusing on race and tribe, and ignoring religion, language and national origin in the equation simplifies the official demarcation of identity under indirect rule in a major way. This applies to natives as well as non-natives. Some examples given in his own book and a cursory perusal of the census reports in colonial East Africa reveal the weakness of his depictions. The population in British East Africa was, in terms of all aspects of life, divided into three racial groupings, European, Asian and Arab, and African. If you visited a bank, you would find European managers, Asian clerks and cashiers, and African cleaners. The Africans were divided in terms of tribe and religion. For example, the Christian areas that grew export crops had better educational facilities than the Muslim areas that supplied migrant labor for plantations. Representing a reversal from the era of German rule, this became a source of friction that persists to this day. Among the Asians, only the economically dominant and politically well-connected Ismaili religious community was permitted to set up its own exclusive system of education. In pursuit of a simple conceptual cogency based on race and tribe, Mamdani presents a shallow picture of a complex reality in which administrative groupings were formed from a judicious blend of existent and constructed identities.

Mamdani's principal weakness stems from his almost total abandonment of economic issues. Yet, some of the scholars who feature extensively in this book do invoke them. Henry Maine opined that the caste system in India was but a religiously sanctioned rationalization for economic and class divisions (p 13). In that vein, Mamdani could have declared that the separation of natives and settlers under colonial rule was but a political and cultural veil for egregious economic stratification. He would then have echoed the forebodings of his hero, Julius Nyerere, on the potent overlap between race and economic privilege in that era.

Bela Usman brings neo-colonialism into the picture in his analysis of tribal identity and notes the effect of emergence of a market economy on identity formation in Africa. And there are other relevant instances from this work. Is it then justified to completely leave out economic factors and neo-colonialism from an analysis of national identity in post-colonial Africa? How did the initial attainments and subsequent abject failure of the post-colonial economic policies affect the strengthening and/or weakening of the nascent sense of national identity? Did the commonality of economic problems and foes of African nations, as noted by progressive scholars like Rodney, contribute to the enhancement of a pan-African identity? If not, why not? What was the contribution of Frantz Fanon on the settler/native divide and identity formation in colonial and post-colonial Africa? For Mamdani, these are irrelevant queries. Particularly, when formulating the basis of his stand on identity, he assiduously avoids economic issues.

The final portion of Mamdani's monograph deals with how Julius Nyerere went about 'creating an inclusive citizenship and building a nation-state' in mainland Tanzania after Independence (p 108). That is done because Nyerere's endeavors represent 'the most successful attempt to dismantle the structures of indirect rule through sustained but peaceful reform' in Africa (p 107).

We learn how Nyerere systematically dismantled the tribe based system of local administration, and replaced it with a unified system based on national laws. Further, in the face of opposition from racially oriented politicians, he managed to enact citizenship laws that did not differentiate people on the basis of skin colour. While Mamdani presents a decent case for these two issues, it has two glaring flaws. It leaves out two singularly pertinent issues, namely, religion and Zanzibar.

With Islam and Christianity the dominant, numerically almost equal faiths in the nation, at Independence, the Muslims felt that they had been at greater disadvantage under colonial rule and sought specific measures to redress the situation. Nyerere was not as successful in bridging this divide. It rumbled on beneath the surface throughout his tenure, and, to this day, many Muslims feel, rightly or wrongly, that Nyerere was 'anti-Muslim' (Hirji 2014b; Maoulidi 2009; Said 2014).

Not dealing with Zanzibar permits Mamdani to posit the army mutiny of 1964 as the most important challenge faced by Nyerere. The role of violence in the creation of Tanzania and the vexing matter of fairness and equality for the citizens of one part of Tanzania are then side lined. The structure of the union between Zanzibar and mainland Tanzania gives almost free reign to the island authorities to violently suppress, with the help of union armed forces, the voices and electoral will of the people. But for Mamdani, this key aspect of Nyerere's legacy does not exist.

With the scene aptly sanitized, Mamdani applies his simple model of race and tribe. Yet, even in that exercise, because he dispenses with relevant economic matters, applies a homogenized picture of Asians in the nation, forgets about neo-colonialism and the nature of the neo-colonial state, his conclusions remain highly suspect.

At Independence, people of Asian origin had two years within which to apply for citizenship. At the outset, most of them were undecided. Interestingly, it was the Ismaili community, the most favored by colonial rule, that took the initiative. Its members acquired citizenship in droves and, in the next five years, significantly expanded their commercial and industrial ventures. Yet a decade on, that picture was turned upside down. After the state acquisition of commercial properties in 1971, it was this community that led the way in the mass exodus of Asians from Tanzania. Today, the Ismailis form a small portion of a much-dwindled number of Asians in Tanzania. And about a fifth of them today are recent non-citizen arrivals from India and Pakistan. What were the causes — economic, religious and political – behind this historic shift? Because Mamdani posits a unitary, passive Asian community, and as that weakens his case for the successful integration of non-natives into the independent nation, and also, as it concerns factors he deems marginal, Mamdani purges such issues from history. Furthermore, he fails to note the resurgence of racial exclusivism and intolerance in the neo-liberal times, which point to the weaknesses of the reforms of the Nyerere era.

Unsurprisingly then, Mamdani as well makes no mention of the large-scale nationalization of banks, industries and other enterprises, foreign and local, that occurred after 1967. Justified or not, overnight state acquisition of private property signifies the use of the coercive power of the state. Why were such measures taken? Posing this question brings into question the depiction of Nyerere as a statesman exclusively occupied with the creation of politically and legally unified nation. But having reached that conclusion from the (surely biased) self-evaluations done by Nyerere after retirement, Mamdani has no cause to venture into the messy realities of history. He can ignore the cogent, empirically grounded analyses of scholars like Adhu Awiti, Andrew Coulson, Henry Mapolu, John Loxley, Walter Rodney, Justinian Rweyemamu, John Saul, Issa Shivji, Tamas Szentes, Michaela von Freyhold and others including the Mahmood Mamdani of yesterday who revealed a different way of interpreting those events. Though, a reason is provided for that omission: These are but leftist 'critics [who] contemptuously dismissed [Ujamaa] as a romantic and unscientific endeavour' (p 108). What more needs to be said?

But one thing Mamdani is unable to ignore is the villagization scheme implemented under Nyerere. It transported, in a chaotic but generally brutal manner, some ten million rural residents into *Ujamaa* villages. He concedes that such actions weaken the designation of Nyerere's reforms as purely non-violent. But we get the impression from Mamdani that such a mode of operation was an aberration from Nyerere's normally peaceful style. One cannot but admire the adroit word play that permits Mamdani to view the herding millions of people into new villages as not a central, defining aspect of Nyerere's statecraft. But since he also forgets the frequent, uncalled-for deployment of the riot police unit inherited from the colonial rulers to suppress numerous student and worker protests throughout the Nyerere era, Mamdani can safely pursue his binary, identity based analysis.

Interestingly, in two end notes, Mamdani discloses in small print that the system of administration under which the *Ujamaa* villages were to function was designed by a major US consultancy company and that subsequently, all regional development planning was assigned to agencies from 'donor' nations on a region by region basis. Yet, those facts form a part of a veritable mountain of evidence collected by progressive scholars that establish the neo-colonial, dependency generating character of the economic policies pursued under Nyerere.

Selectivity of evidence allows Mamdani to put forth the proposition that Nyerere primarily was concerned about building a centrally unified nation state, and not about constructing a society based on economic equality and development for all. Is Mamdani now dismissing *Ujamaa* 'as a romantic and unscientific endeavor'? That anomaly aside, he is on shaky grounds. Nyerere sought to attain both the goals. Even a cursory look at the policy documents and governmental and party actions of that era suffices to establish that nationalizations, creation of *Ujamaa* villages, the new educational policy, the leadership code, and calls for self-reliance formed a strategy aimed at elimination of exploitation of humans by humans and creation of a just society with prosperity for all.

That strategy was derailed soon after inception. Eventually, it ended as a failure of monumental proportions. It is a complex tale. In sum, the faults stemmed from not tackling the external dependency, remaining within the purview of the World Bank inspired economic prescriptions, reliance on a neo-colonial state apparatus, the influence of a petty bourgeois ruling party and the dominance, in day-to-day operations, of a self-centered, greedy bureaucracy. In the end, the policy did more harm than good.

After his retirement, Nyerere did not give an adequate accounting of what happened during the 25 years of his rule. His speeches and writings noted a few failures but mainly highlighted his accomplishments. Mamdani unduly relies on these subjective declarations but does not give due weight to the totality of historical evidence. His conclusions thus not only embody the personal bias of a politician but, at times, reverse cause and effect.

More can be said, but what has been said suffices to show that Mamdani employs a defective method to analyze history and society, and resorts to partial evidence to arrive at weighty conclusions. There is no question that Julius Nyerere was a humble man, a dedicated Pan-Africanist and a humanist who towered head and shoulders above the despotic, avaricious tyrants who ruled Africa in his days. But that is no reason to place him on a pedestal and not subject his rule to a thorough critical inquiry. And he was not alone. Kenneth Kaunda of Zambia was also in that club.

A defining feature of a scholar is the ability to critique one's own ideas and evolve along the intellectual front. Such an evolution, however, should not reflect expediency or change for the sake of it. Especially if a scholar changes his or her basic world view in a major way, it should be accompanied with a clear explanation of why that has been done. Yet, other than taking cheap pot shots at Marxism, Mamdani has not provided an adequate rationale for why he jumped from one end of the socio-analytic horizon to another. Has he disavowed his own stellar works of the yesteryears? Mamdani thus he stands in the company of the bulk of modern day historians of Africa who can go no further than distort and superficially critique the works and Marxist approach of Walter Rodney. He surely ought to heed the advice a historian he strongly admires:

> The more important question [is] how to detect and deal with one's own bias. Bala Usman (cited on p 89).

## IMPLICATIONS

The main implications of my evaluation of Mamdani's framework defining monograph are as follows:

First, as noted in the previous chapter, nowadays most historians writing on Africa agree that economic factors constituted, in policy and practice, the primary drivers of colonial rule. By his compartmentalized ejection of economics from history, Mamdani takes us back to a retrogressive era of conceptualizing history.

Secondly, like Ali Mazrui, Mamdani has mastered the flowery art of saying the same thing in a creative multiplicity of ways. It gives an impression of profundity and novelty where there is neither. Terminology aside, the main principles of his historiography and take on identity, citizenship and nationhood mirror the similarly focused but superficial, selective and distorted works on Africa emanating from the Western academia today. For the case of Tanzania, see Aminzade (2013), Brenan (2012), Fouere (20015) and Ivaska (2011).

Thirdly, Mamdani's vision of Africa is an amalgam of the political-cultural Africanism of Ali Mazrui with the humanism of Julius K Nyerere. Yet, as it distorts the economic realities of Africa, and ignores class analysis and imperialism, it is fundamentally inimical to the interests of the people of Africa.

Fourthly, the great men theory of history states that the course of history is determined by exceptional individuals: emperors, generals, geniuses and the like. Today, few historians subscribe to it. Yet, the depiction of the role of Julius Nyerere in pre- and post-Independence Tanzania given by Mamdani revives that mode of thinking. He fails to accord due weight to the local and Africa-wide contextual and historical factors that affected the changes that occurred in the nation. These include: an indigenous national language, absence of strongly competing ethnic groups, a small number of metropolitan settlers, absence of wide scale land alienation, high level of cooperation between the two major religious communities and the way the anti-colonial struggle evolved from the early days. While Mamdani mentions the ultra-nationalistic leaders who differed with Nyerere, he pays no attention to the scores of prominent and hundreds of grassroots level leaders who saw eye to eye with him. It is as if one great man, by himself, determined what occurred in Tanzania (Said 2014). And it is this failure to see Nyerere as a representative of an emergent social class that also limits, as shown below, his ability to explain the long run trajectory of that nation.

To assess the comparative appropriateness of Rodney's political economy-based approach and Mahmood Mamdani's identity-based approach for dealing with Africa's modern day problems, we remain in

Tanzania, and examine the present situation in this nation where both of them spent nearly seven years of their early academic careers, and where their stays overlapped for three of those years.

## TANZANIA TODAY

Like most African nations, Tanzania in the 1980s was compelled to adopt the structural adjustment program decreed by the IMF and World Bank. Its main conditions were reduction in state outlays for administration, social services and subsidies, and curtailment of state involvement in the economy. Higher education was one of the first areas to feel the axe.

The process gained momentum at the onset of the neoliberal era in the 1990s. Publicly owned banks, industries, transport firms, import/export agencies, wholesale and retail trade companies, agricultural marketing organizations and cooperative unions, mines, hotels, housing stock etc., were dismantled or sold off to private buyers on a massive scale. Many rural health centers ceased operation. Teachers, civil servants and health workers by the thousands became jobless overnight. New laws that protected employers and private property, but disadvantaged workers, tenants and rural small holders were enacted.

Privatization was a corrupt exercise implemented hastily with no regard for the national interest. The principal beneficiaries were foreign companies, local business groups and the upper echelon of the state bureaucracy (Sharife 2009). Private firms that had purchased state assets at fire-sale prices failed to adhere to the sale conditions. Apart from a few lucrative exceptions, instead of revival and efficient running of ailing state firms, the opposite occurred. Industrial machinery was auctioned-off, factories were converted into warehouses and giant state farms were left idle.

Implemented alongside trade and financial liberalizations, the results were virtual decimation of the small but significant manufacturing sector built over four decades, loss of vital institutional skills, and inundation of the market by cheap, low quality imports. Instead of processed or semi-processed exports, raw lower value goods were sold abroad. Urban unemployment and rural to urban migration rose rapidly.

This transformation formed the basis for the emergence of a two-tier society: *wananchi* (people of the nation) and *wenyenchi* (masters of the nation). While abuse of public funds had been endemic for decades, in the neo-liberal era, it reached astronomical proportions. Embezzlement, fraud, sweet-heart deals and under-the-table pay outs from foreign and local companies seeking special terms converted bureaucrats into multi-millionaires. Some built their own business, transport and real estate empires. On the other hand, more and more street kids, beggars and aimless youth were seen plying the city streets.

That the neoliberal 'reforms' were socially deleterious and potentially destabilizing was apparent by the end of the decade. Some backtracking was necessary. The Western agencies goaded the pliant African rulers to adopt a new set of remedial measures: the Millennium Development Goals. The stress was on education, health and social services placed under state and NGO management. Cost sharing was partly curtailed. Most projects relied heavily on external funds. Significant issues like food self-sufficiency, unemployment, inter-regional trade, small scale industries, and economic self-determination were, however, not on the agenda. The talk was of youth and female empowerment.

By 2010, the achievements of some of the externally financed projects, especially in education, looked remarkable. But it was more in quantity, not quality. To attain enrolment targets, thousands of primary level classrooms were built. School attendance shot up, yet pupils had few teachers and no books or desks. Though things have begun to improve of recent, the quality of education for the majority of children in primary, secondary and tertiary educational institutions is as low as it was in the colonial era. Such education does not get you a worthwhile job. Employers routinely complain that university graduates with impressive transcripts are unable to communicate adequately in Swahili or English, and cannot perform basic tasks without close supervision (Kolumbia 2016). Yet, the children of the elite attend costly private schools where they get education of the type prevalent in Western nations. Inequality in access to health service is more striking. The feverish child of a domestic worker does not get malaria medication priced less than US $1 in a public facility while senior officials and upper class persons go to India and South Africa for routine medical check-up that costs thousands of dollars. Progress in public health is paradoxical. One survey indicates a dramatic fall in childhood mortality but another points to a high and rising childhood malnutrition rate. These surveys lack adequate quality control mechanisms. The high and increasing prevalence of obesity, diabetes, and cardio-vascular conditions is a major concern.

Extreme economic and social inequality is an accompaniment of the pervasive external dependency in all sectors: industry, transport, trade, finance, education, health, welfare programs, and even culture and sports (Mazanza 2016).

An incident that revealed the extent of external dependency occurred during the visit of the then President Jakaya Kikwete to Australia in 2014. At the university where he was given an award for achievements in the health sector, he was regaled by an Australian singer with a moving rendition of his nation's iconic patriotic song: *Tanzania, Tanzania*. Sung in a pitch-perfect Swahili style, the way a native speaker of the language would, her voice, tonality and the accompanying music were mesmerizing. At the end, the President went to congratulate her and said: 'You do it better than we do.' But when he returned home, he was not asked why they represent our culture better than we do, or to what degree were his policies responsible for that state of affairs. The Swahili music and song heard on the Tanzanian radio and TV stations is either religious or the Western-type high-beat variety with grizzly, morally dubious, lyrics. The English songs are of the same style. The rich, vast cultural heritage from the 60s and 70s has all but disappeared. *Tanzania, Tanzania* is heard once in a blue. In the past, the government and public enterprises sponsored a plethora of music bands, singers and cultural activities. They were also given plenty of airtime. Today, such practices are a rarity. Non-commercial local cultural groups are highly dependent on external sponsors. Even pointing out the simple fact that Mount Kilimanjaro has the tallest trees in Africa has been left to foreign researchers (The Citizen 2016b).

External agencies initiate, fund and micro-manage thousands of projects across all sectors. It is a largely uncoordinated process. You find the ambassadors, NGO heads and dignitaries from Norway to the UK, from the USA to Japan visiting villages, schools, health centers and water projects they have funded. Like the colonial officials of the past, they are received with fanfare and gratitude by the ordinary people. They are seen as the saviors, unlike the uncaring, corrupt district and regional bosses. External agents influence the drafting of important laws and adoption of a new constitution.

Scenes sadly reminiscent of the docile subservience of the colonial era, unthinkable in the days of Nyerere, are an accepted part of the socio-political landscape. The adulation with which US presidents Bill Clinton, George Bush and Barak Obama were welcomed here illustrates that tendency. The airspace came under US control and senior local officials were frisked and sniffed by dogs humiliatingly as if they were terrorists. As crowds danced and waved the American flag, the media projected the image of a benefactor descended from heaven. The main complaint was that people were not allowed to get close to the eminent dignitary.

Such scenes reflect a 180-degrees turnaround in the nation's historic frontline stand against colonial domination. Tanzania under Nyerere had backed the struggles of the peoples of Western Sahara and Palestine for self-determination, and had hosted their representatives. In 2016, even though Morocco had shown no signs of budging from the territory it has occupied, the King of Morocco was in Tanzania for a state visit and was received with fanfare. The two nations signed twenty-one economic and cultural agreements. Since the year 2000, many Israeli companies have begun operations in Tanzania. Apart from some Islamic outlets, the print and broadcast media, state and private, have a pro-Israel slant. On the diplomatic front, Tanzania and Croatia were the two nations that helped, at a major UNESCO forum, the passage of a resolution on the status of Jerusalem favored by Israel. While on a visit to Israel, the speaker of the Tanzanian parliament paid a courtesy call to his counterpart in the Knesset. Yet, the Palestinian ambassador to Tanzania had to wait for more than six months to talk to officials in the Ministry of Foreign Affairs. While Nyerere stood for East African unity, the government of Tanzania now expresses strong reservations about moving that process forward. These are but a few instances of new political landscape that generate little critical comment.

President Magufuli, elected in 2015, has embarked on a major drive to curb the abuse and misuse of state resources and control tax evasion. It has uncovered financial scandals, bribery, frivolous expenses, fraud, lack of work discipline and mismanagement on a scale too shocking even to the most cynical observer. A massive clean-up of bad officials and practices has ensued. Government offices, public hospitals and the public education system now operate more efficiently.

The key question thereupon is: What next? The official answer is to stick to the neo-liberal agenda, but implement it more efficiently and on terms more favourable to Tanzania. No bold, innovative development plan is on the horizon.

Take a central concern: Creation of jobs, especially for the youth, and skilled jobs that pay well, is one of the weakest features of the economy. Pronouncements about a major industrialization drive have been issued. But inquiry reveals that no plan or state run scheme exists. The task has been left entirely to the private, mainly foreign, firms that will be afforded tax and other incentives to encourage them to invest here. The recently opened factories are capital intensive with the bulk of the labor force getting a very low wage. In addition, of recent, many private industries are closing shop.

Dealing with job creation for the youth has been farmed out to external entities. The Obama Youth Initiative run by USAID, the multi-institutional Ready to Work Plan funded by Barclays Bank, and the Via-Pathways Project supported by the MasterCard Foundation, among several such projects, are expected to place millions Tanzanian youth into gainful work (Lamtey 2016; Lawi 2016; Tungaraza 2016). Yet, despite the hype, most of them do not involve much more than teaching entrepreneurship and computer skills, which is supplemented by standard motivational lectures.

Very low wage in highly profitable enterprises, besides its adverse impact on family life and health, fails to generate the purchasing power for stimulating sustainable development. In the growing tourism sector, for example, there are international brand hotels, beach resorts and safari lodges that charge US $200 to US $300 per night. But the kitchen, cleaning and serving staff are lucky to be paid US $5 per day. Within the past two decades, the city of Dar es Salaam has been transformed by a multitude of impressive high rise structures that house state and corporate offices, luxury apartments, fancy restaurants, costly places of entertainment and Western style shops for the wealthy. The monthly rental for a two-bedroom flat exceeds what a primary school teacher earns in a year. The common man either does a menial job at the place or just admires it from outside. Limitations of space does not permit giving more examples, but suffice to say that the set up reminds one of Fanon's contrasting descriptions of the town of the settlers and the town of the natives.

Extreme and growing social and economic inequality, pervasive external dependency and worship of everything Western have frayed the strong sense of national identity that developed during the Nyerere era. The feeling that we are in the same boat has all but vanished. The opposition political parties and the private and state media are as well wedded to the neo-liberal program and worship of things Western. A few parties have ties with right wing groups in the West. The lack of meaningful alternatives makes the politicians fall back on narrow loyalties. The frustrated public is quite receptive to the divisive rhetoric of the demagogic politicians. Hence we see rising tensions along racial, religious, regional and ethnic lines in this hitherto largely peaceful nation (Hirji 2014a).

The state in Tanzania retains the essential features of the state set up in the colonial times. It services global multinational companies and their local allies, and protects a system that subjugates the masses. That is the feature it shares with the state in Kenya, Uganda, South Africa or Egypt. Indeed, there are political, legal and security related differences. While such differences are important, we cannot ignore the shared class based features. In the current historic juncture, dependent neo-liberal states operate, in the economy, politics and societal affairs, in a fairly uniform manner not just in Africa but on the planet as a whole. And it is a mode of operation that decisively and adversely impinges on popular struggles for justice, economic welfare, democracy, equality, social tranquility and dignity.

The centrality of economic problems and economic inequality and their connection with the spectacular rise in religious extremism, xenophobia, racial intolerance, suspicion of outsiders, nationalistic paranoia, uncivil behavior, and tendency to violently deal with fellow humans is visible across the planet. People everywhere are disaffected by the *status quo*. The events and political outcomes in South Africa, India, the Philippines, Eastern and Western Europe, the UK (Brexit) and USA (Trumpism) should leave us in no doubt about that. Unfortunately, popular anger is exploited by fascistic and fundamentalist movements to enhance their political clout. It is a path to civil strife, fascism and reckless wars.

Economic factors and trends are strong drivers of identity formation, the sense of a common nationhood and human solidarity, in a positive or negative sense. In time, narrow divisiveness can assume a momentum of its own. This is what Rodney's political-economy based approach teaches us. And that is exactly what Mamdani's identity driven approach fails to capture.

### A NEW VISION

That not just the political class but even the prominent intellectuals of Africa today are gripped by outlooks that sit well with the imperialist overlords of the continent and cause but minor discomfort to its greedy rulers points to the continued indispensability of the mode of thought championed by Walter Rodney and his compatriots. We need to move beyond the narrative of citizenship, corruption, electoral democracy and human rights, and think in terms of elimination of exploitation and dependency, promoting grass roots democracy, building a society based on equality and social justice, and firm promotion of people-based Pan-Africanism.

Not putting the economic plight of the people at the center stage, not shining a sustained bright light on the systemic, systematic, persistent and intense economic exploitation of African land, labor and resources, and endlessly engaging in verbal acrobatics with secondary ideas like direct and indirect rule and their consequences is precisely what the imperialists and their lackeys prefer. Were he with us, it is exactly what Rodney would loudly bring to our attention: 'Brothers and sisters, they came to rob us, they have robbed us for centuries, and in a dirty alliance with the modern day local stooges, they want to go on doing it in perpetuity.' He would thunder and urge us to 'keep our eyes on the prize.' I have no doubt that on this score, he would argue with Professor Mamdani today as surely and vigorously as he did with Professor Mazrui in the 1970s.

Rodney would educate us that those who perpetuate the view that 'Nowadays African leaders, not the outsiders, are underdeveloping Africa' are telling but one side of the story. The exclusive focus on those who rob by the millions protects the external hegemons who rob by the billions. Such voices are either oblivious of the strategic alliance between the local political and business elites and the imperialists, or they simply seek NGO funds from the masters.

The choice for the people in Africa and everywhere is clear: Fascism, divisiveness and violence **or** socialism, solidarity and social tranquility. It is time to dispense with the elusive notions of identity and seriously consider the visionary ideas of Walter Rodney and his compatriots that not only better explain the realities of today but as well point a realistic, humanistic way out of the global malaise.

CHAPTER 9

## HOPE AND STRUGGLE

Walter Rodney was not the first, only, or last person to apply the Marxist approach to unravel the history of Africa. He stood on the shoulders of giants. But as an intellectual, he too became a giant, a highly influential giant. He did not approach history like an accountant producing a balance sheet. Instead of a pros and cons style, he adopted a systemic method that sought to unveil, within an interdisciplinary perspective, the short and long term dynamics of societal change. His approach did not target or blame races, nations or religions. Instead, he looked for explanations in the context of an evolving global capitalist system, the tentacles it set up in Africa and the resultant consequences for the continent and its peoples.

My diary says that I first met Walter Rodney on July 10, 1969 at the University of Dar es Salaam. He had just given a lecture on *The Cuban Revolution and its Relevance to Africa* to a packed audience of students and staff. It was sponsored by the University Students African Revolutionary Front (USARF) – a socialist, Pan-Africanist student organization of which I was a member. A few comrades had stayed behind to meet with him.

We had had discussions about Cuba in the USARF study groups, read Fidel Castro and Che Guevara, and the Cuban magazine *Granma*. Nevertheless, our knowledge of its revolutionary process was still shallow. We knew events and personalities, but not the reality beneath the surface.

Walter sketched the background, identified the critical signposts, gave illuminating details, and set the global context in an integrated but clear manner. His captivating metallic voice and lyrical style transfixed the audience. He made us laugh and ponder at the same time. His exposition of US imperialism made the case for the essential relevance of the Cuban experience to Africa unimpeachable. I am sure that that evening Walter won over many wavering student minds to the cause of African liberation.

Before going to bed that night, I wrote in my diary:

> The most impressive and brilliant speech I have heard so far. One could almost feel the strong conviction and deep emotions from which he spoke. I am convinced that Comrade Rodney is one of the most devoted and brilliant socialists to be found anywhere (Karim Hirji, 10 July 1969).

First impressions are reputed to mislead. In this instance, the opposite was the case. This first impression hit the nail right on its head. Over the following six years, I learned, struggled and laughed with this wonderful man on many occasions, over a host of issues, and at a close level. Never did I have cause to revise my initial take. It is thus with a sense of honor that, in this concluding chapter, I present my remembrances of a titan of the human race and the lessons about the struggle for human dignity and emancipation he has left for us.

First I recollect a few personal interactions. Then I outline the socio-political context of those days. Thereafter, I discuss the contradiction between hope and struggle as it affected the building of socialism in Tanzania, relate how Walter Rodney dealt with it over the course of his stay in that country, and explain its contemporary import.

The contradiction between hope and struggle, in its general form, pertains to the strivings for a just, humane, non-militaristic, non-corporate, egalitarian social order everywhere. I argue that we have much to learn from the way Walter Rodney formulated, navigated and resolved it in a specific instance.

## WALTER THE MAN

Three months after I met him, I was elected the senior editor of *Cheche*, the new USARF magazine. As we scoured around for articles, he readily agreed to write one. Not only did he keep his word, but his article was the first ever submission for *Cheche*. And it was directly typed on stencils, saving us much trouble (Rodney 1969a). He handed me the stencils near the student cafeteria – the scene lingers in my mind, and I still have those now frayed, barely legible stencils.

Walter became a key contributor to this student run magazine and its successor, *MajiMaji*. His trenchant, analytic pieces did not shy away from controversy. They were a major attraction for students, academics, and people beyond the campus. The quality, circulation and reputation of the radical, but resource-deprived, fledgling magazines were well promoted by the presence of his amply researched articles.

Walter was an associate member of USARF (only students could get full membership). He gave lectures in the Sunday USARF self-education classes, participated in sweat drenching work in cooperative villages and student-run farms, attended symposiums, demonstrations and exhibitions about the war in Vietnam, the struggle against Portuguese colonial rule and apartheid South Africa, and supported the efforts of the African liberation movements.

This was in addition to the demanding teaching, research and other responsibilities in the History Department. On that front, he challenged, with evidence and keen logic, the biases in the mainstream elaborations of global and African histories. It was not to the liking of reactionary social scientists, Tanzanian and expatriate, but among the students, he was a distinctively admired and popular teacher.

Since I was majoring in mathematics, I was not formally enrolled in his history courses. But I learned a lot from my continual interactions with him outside the classroom. A high point on that front was when he asked Henry Mapolu, a *Cheche* co-editor and sociology major, and me to comment on the draft chapters of *HEUA*. To this day, I boast that I was among the very first persons to read what has become a classic of African history. I remember the three of us sitting down week after week, two to three hours at a time, discussing one chapter after next in the close confines of the USARF office.

Henry and I were influenced by Andre Gunder Frank's theory of underdevelopment. But our understanding was of a mechanistic variety. Walter provided the complexity and dynamics. We critiqued the lower emphasis on internal struggles. The towering historian patiently paid attention to the two upstart students, and, in places, revised what he had written. Without doubt, those sessions were the best lessons in history I have ever had.

When the aptly sized book came out a year on, we proudly carried it around in the same spirit as the Chinese youth carried around the pocket book of quotations of Chairman Mao!

But it was not all work and work. Walter interacted with us on a personal basis too. We went to his place, played with his children, and enjoyed the tasty food Pat Rodney served us. Once, two months or so after we had gotten married, Farida and I were at a party in his place. On the social front, I had a reserved personality. As the party got swinging, Farida and I sat in a corner, whispering to ourselves. When Walter observed us, he marched to us forthwith and pronounced loudly, 'The two of you need to separate.' With that he took Farida by the hand and set her amidst one vibrant group, and then, with a wink, hauled me off to another.

Two years earlier, I was set to depart for postgraduate study at the London School of Economics. My family, Joe Kanywanyi and Haroub Othman were at the airport to bid me *safari njema* (safe trip). In those hot-headed days, it was taboo for me to put on a formal dress. But my father said that I could not go to London looking like a 'vagabond.' So he purchased a suit, tie and associated stuff. At his insistence, I put them on.

When Walter arrived and saw me dandily attired, he elicited a loud laugh. 'Karim, Cabral says the petty bourgeoisie need to commit suicide,' (A reference to the Guinea Bissau freedom fighter Amilcar Cabral's call to the elite in Africa to abandon the get-rich-quick mentality and facile imitation of Western culture, and dedicate itself to serve the masses), he said as he thumped me on the back, 'But what I see here is a petty bourgeois rebirth!' I cherish a picture of that episode (see Photo). When I look at it, I recall his jest with a smile.

Talking of elitism, I had one misgiving. Walter was enamored with cricket. He attended cricket matches and played the game. But in Tanzania, it was an exclusive sport. Most teams were parochial, representing the different segments of the Asian business community. Among the audience or players, hardly any black faces were seen. Why did he go to such elitist events? Reasoning that no one is perfect, and that it was but a minor transgression, I did not raise the issue.

It is only when I read CLR James' majestic rendition of cricket in the West Indies that I came to realize how misguided I had been. In that part of the world, cricket, though a colonial import, was internalized into the local culture and had become a pastime of the masses. It also was a vehicle for the expression of nationalistic sentiment (James 1993). Walter's predilection towards cricket reflected that socio-historic reality, not elitism. Seek the meaning of an act, as they say, not in the abstract but in the social context in which it occurs.

## UJAMAA IN TANZANIA

Now I outline the political scene of this period. Under the leadership of Mwalimu Nyerere, Tanzania adopted the policy of Socialism and Self-Reliance. Banks, industries, firms, and plantations were nationalized, rural development was promoted under collective villages, the education system was overhauled, and a code to restrict the accumulation of wealth by the political elite was instituted. Guidelines for worker self-management and local control in the rural areas were promulgated. All this fell under the rubric of the policy of *Ujamaa* (Nyerere 1967; TANU 1967; TANU 1971).

The masses at home and progressive forces abroad hailed these moves. Coming on top of a firm anti-colonial foreign policy, they gained wide international acclaim for the nation. Reactionary African leaders, Western media and the imperialists, however, spared no vitriol for what Mwalimu Nyerere said and did.

Progressive students and academic staff at UDSM were in full support of anti-colonialism, socialism and Pan-Africanism. We promoted these ideas in words and deeds. We studied the theoretical aspects of *Ujamaa*, and examined how it was implemented. We investigated how it affected the lives of the workers, peasants, teachers and common folk. Public discussions and written debates on what we observed took place.

The September 1970 special issue of *Cheche* was devoted to a pioneering paper by Issa Shivji entitled *Tanzania: The Silent Class Struggle*. He subsequently expanded his analysis in *Tanzania: The Class Struggle Continues* (Shivji 1970;1973;1976). These works scrutinized *Ujamaa* in practice and the emergent socio-economic trends in Tanzania. An extensive outpouring of research and analyses relating to the condition of workers, life in rural areas, health and education policies, agriculture and industrialization projects, development planning, and so on by others also occurred. Some details and references are in Hirji (2011) and Coulson (1979;2014).

## TWO TENDENCIES

The voluminous research and analyses by progressive scholars presented an unmistakable message: there was a large gap between the theory and practice of *Ujamaa*. Whether in rural or urban areas, agriculture, tourism or industry, education or social services, colonial era tendencies persisted. Unplanned, counterproductive implementation was the norm, and new forms of bureaucratic domination were emerging. Key institutions were public in name only as they were dominated by Western capitalist entities and modes of action. Ordinary people were marginalized and bore the brunt of the ensuing economic and social chaos. Investigations by astute mainstream scholars conveyed essentially the same message. The benefits of the new policy were, apart from a few demonstration cases, limited in time, place and extent.

Such revelations generated two basic modes of thought among the progressive students and staff. I will call them the tendency of hope and the tendency of struggle.

The former argued that despite the observed problems, there were other factors and forces that made attainment of socialism under the existing framework a realistic possibility. The gap between the haves and have-nots was much smaller in Tanzania than elsewhere in the Third World. Landlessness and similar societal ills were less extreme. The country was stable and unified, culturally and politically, unlike most African nations. And most importantly, Mwalimu Nyerere was a genuinely committed, honest and enlightened leader, respected by the nation at large. The errors in implementing *Ujamaa* would thereby be a springboard from which lessons would be learned, and the nation put on the desired path.

In other words, there was great room for hope. The progressives should rally behind Mwalimu Nyerere, mobilize support for his policies at the grassroots level, and isolate the reactionary forces in the ruling party and the state. Extreme conditions like those in Latin America that bred armed rebellions were not only non-existent, but, given the trends, were also unlikely in Tanzania.

The tendency of hope is exemplified in a speech given by the respected Caribbean Marxist and Pan-Africanist CLR James. He deemed Julius Nyerere a practical socialist who thoroughly understood the problems facing Africa. In his estimation, Nyerere stood shoulder to shoulder with Lenin in confronting the challenging problems of the peasantry. On the question of education, his assessment is worth a quote:

> [T]here is one of the most important features of political development in the world today, not only for the underdeveloped countries but, I am positive, I have examined it, the advanced countries, in their systems of education in particular, have a lot to learn from what is taking place in Tanzania (James 1973).

The tendency of struggle accepted that the intense, Latin America-type of contradictions were not present in Tanzania. But it noted that all the trends in the economy and state organizations were in an anti-socialist direction. Socialism had become a cover for policies inspired by the World Bank. The rural decentralization scheme enacted in 1972 ensued from a report produced by a major American management consultancy firm. Imagine Fidel Castro calling upon a US multinational to guide the rural policy in Cuba! Yet, that was what was happening here. Despite the call for self-reliance, Tanzania became among the top recipient of foreign funds in Africa. The funders called the shots in key aspects of development policies.

This tendency showed that despite Mwalimu's commitment, the existing trends were entrenching neo-colonial domination of the economy, political control of the state by the elite, and disempowerment of the masses. If not halted, the future of Tanzania was greater inequality, structural dependency, imperial domination and persistent poverty. It was gradually but consistently on the way to be either a version of state capitalism or a Latin American model state.

Take one case: Henry Mapolu's empirical evaluation of the villagization program reached a firm conclusion – for all the fanfare about cooperative farming, the major outcome was popular disillusionment, and enhanced integration of the peasantry into the global capitalist economy, and that in a condition of further subservience (Mapolu 1986;1990).

The tendency of struggle did not promote armed rebellion. What it called for was independent education and mobilization of the peasants and workers using ways and means that were autonomous, in form and content, from the establishment. The ruling bureaucracy was unlikely to march towards socialism. The essential task was to establish a new political reality through mass mobilization and struggles.

I estimate that the progressive students were about equally divided into the two camps of hope and struggle. Among the progressive academic staff, most of whom were expatriates, the majority favored the hope tendency.

### HOPE OR STRUGGLE?

Like Ernesto Che Guevara, Walter Rodney was a universal being. Outside his home country, he was also at home, keenly immersed in local politics and struggles, and promoting a socialistic agenda in cooperation with local activists. He was not an onlooker, but one of us He engaged in words and deeds, animated heart and soul, with the rough, risky socio-political landscape. Yes, he was grounding with his brothers and sisters.

Earlier I noted some of his activities in local matters at the pedagogic and practical levels. For details, see Alpers and Fontaine (1982), Campbell (1985;1986), Shivji (1993) and Hirji (2011), and the special memorial issue no. 39 of *MajiMaji*. A comprehensive account of his life and work in Tanzania, though, has yet to appear.

My focus is on one matter, namely the discussions on the character of the socialist process in Tanzania. Walter Rodney was a central figure in these debates. In the classroom and beyond, with students and academic staff, in public exchanges and ideological classes, in popular and scholarly writings, he discussed his stand. For example, he and John Saul wrote the two main responses to Issa Shivji's *Silent Class Struggle* (Rodney 1971c; Saul 1971).

I will not render an academic sort of review. My remarks come from my personal interactions with him. After the publication of *Silent Class Struggle*, Walter and I had many one-to-one sessions, some lasting hours, discussing this question. I remember one occasion when we kept Ted Jones, the fabulous African American poet, waiting as we poured over a thorny matter. Needless to say, meeting the dynamic poet later was an enthralling experience.

At this time, Issa Shivji was in London. I wrote long letters to him to keep him abreast of the situation on the campus and the nation. I also conveyed what I discussed with Walter. One of the letters, dated 20 January 1970, survives to this day.

Walter leaned towards the hope tendency, and I towards the struggle tendency. As I wrote to Issa, the key points underlying his stand were:

1. Socialistically inclined forces under the leadership of Mwalimu Nyerere controlled political power in Tanzania.
2. Economic disengagement from neo-colonial domination was a long process with ups and downs.
3. Rural contradictions and land issues in Tanzania were not as sharp, and the peasantry not as intensely dominated by landlords or multinational firms as elsewhere in the global capitalist system.
4. The current direction of the nation exhibited both positive and negative signs.
5. The progressive section of the political elite was expanding. It would eventually put the nation onto a consistently socialistic direction.
6. Our task was to enhance the progressive forces and work against the reactionary ones, but within the current political set-up.

On points (2) and (3), I generally agreed with him. But on other points, I did not. On (1), I held that the character of the state was essentially what was inherited from the colonial times. On (4), I felt that the negative trends far outweighed the few positive ones. On (5), I partly agreed but felt that his assessment was too optimistic. And, on (6), I stressed independent efforts so as not to be compromised by and sucked into an authoritarian bureaucracy.

The supporters of socialism held such discussions in many venues. They also confronted, verbally, in writing and in public demonstrations, a strong group of camouflaged or overtly anti-socialist organizations and people at all levels in the society.

Walter Rodney did not sit back and hope. He actively promoted socialist ideas, and over time acquired a deep insight into the social and economic set up in Tanzania. His views evolved. His critique of Shivji's *The Class Struggle Continues* faulted some details, but his optimism about the socio-political trends was distinctly tempered:

> In Tanzania, as elsewhere, the strengthening of the state has gone hand in hand with the emergence of privileged classes who themselves depend inordinately on the state machinery for power and accumulation (Rodney 1974).

This was a major change from his earlier, short-lived depiction of

*Ujamaa* as Scientific Socialism (Rodney 1972b). As Walter refined his analysis, our dialogue continued. In early 1974, I was ejected from the university. Though couched as a normal transfer, it was a politically driven banishment to a remote area. Comrades and academics tried to reverse the decision but to no avail. Walter gave me firm moral and practical support during those trying days when Farida was pregnant with her first child.

The last time I met him was just before I headed into the hinterland. His views on socialism in Tanzania retained a modicum of hope. But now he accepted that a reactionary bureaucracy was wresting control of key institutions of the state. From viewing class struggle as a battle of ideas among sections of the petty bourgeoisies, he argued that the actual trends were mostly disheartening. To realize *Ujamaa*, a strident struggle against these tendencies was required (Rodney 1980a).

His last words to me in essence were: 'Comrade, wherever we are, the struggle continues.' He was by then preparing to make a transition in which the struggle on the ground would constitute the dominant aspect of his life. And for conducting that struggle, he chose an arena where he would be most effective. I did not meet him again.

### HOPE AND STRUGGLE

When times are bleak, when socially retrogressive forces run amok, an entity standing up anyhow and anywhere to the powers of the day can inspire hope; indeed, a great deal of hope. That is but a natural reaction. And when one comes from afar, it is easy to misjudge the situation and be more hopeful than need be. One lacks the concrete experiences of the local folk. One is not as versed in the local cultural and social exchange to draw as critical a conclusion as ought to be the case. But being an outsider has its advantages too in that one can be less biased in terms of supporting this or that view on subjective, person-based, or non-evidentiary factors.

Nyerere boldly stood up to Western imperialism like few other African leaders did. He was an honest, decent, intellectually astute, visionary, Pan-Africanist leader. He lived in the era of Mobutu, Banda and Kenyatta. He inspired many. He initiated major changes in his country. No wonder, he generated a great deal of hope, both in the nation and abroad.

This quote by CLR James was a typical instance of the veneration of his policies by far sighted personalities of unimpeachable integrity from Africa and beyond. Yet, 1973 was not 1968. Had James written those words in 1968, I would have stood with him. By 1973, I had had a five-year worth of contact with many schools – in teaching practice, as a supervisor of trainees in teaching practice, as a speaker before student groups, in contacts with numerous teachers, and as an informal visitor. My assessment of Education for Self-Reliance concluded the opposite of what James states. In virtually all schools, among teachers and students, it was an unpopular policy. It was implemented in a haphazard manner and was blamed for lowering the standard of education (Hirji 1973; Mbilinyi 1979). And it was essentially for writing those critical words that I was banished from the university.

CLR James gave several inspiring speeches at the UDSM in 1968. I was in the audience. But his views remained static. Perhaps he had too many things in mind. But, without detracting from his profound contribution to our understanding of the situation in the Third World, I say with confidence that by 1973 his take on education in Tanzania was way off the mark.

At the outset, Walter Rodney and CLR James had similar stands on socialism in Tanzania. But unlike his erstwhile mentor, Walter's stand was a dynamic one. He learned from practice. He paid attention to the facts, the life of the common person and the views of other comrades. He exuded the humility and intellectual honesty that a person genuinely dedicated to social transformation ought to possess.

Just after Walter Rodney was assassinated, CLR James critiqued him on the question of state power (James 1981). He had some valid points. But a while back, James had also dealt with that question in Tanzania in a superficial way. He did not note that fact. Nor did he admit that Rodney had eventually come to a more valid analysis of state power in Tanzania.

**CONTEMPORARY IMPORT**

Hope and struggle are fundamental to striving for social (or personal) change. No movement can flourish without both. The question is what aspect dominates at what point in time, and where to draw the line so as not to be side tracked or get stuck in a morass.

Take the case of the progressive forces in the USA: the workers, immigrants, women, Native Americans, oppressed communities like African Americans and Hispanic Americans, and the anti-war and social justice groups. The past fifty years show that when the president is a Republican, they are energized, come out on the streets and struggle for change. But when a Democrat is in the White House, their expectations are so raised that most community based struggles come to a halt or are suspended. That the Democrat, without exception, implements what is essentially the Republican economic, foreign policy, military, educational and other agendas is overlooked or downplayed.

When he raised basic economic and anti-war issues, Martin Luther

King faced criticism from those who had hope in the establishment. The same thing happened to progressive activists who maintained their critical stands under Bill Clinton and Obama (Comissiong 2012; Ford 2012).

That dilemma prevailed in the Arab Spring as well. At the outset, it was a progressive, local liberation movement. But then it was hijacked. The forces of struggle placed undue reliance on Western entities that previously propped up the regime. But others proclaimed that there was little hope for fundamental change through cooperation with these imperial powers (Beckett 2009; Smulewitz-Zucker and Thompson 2015; Traboulsi 2012).

The same problem exists regarding regimes like those of Robert Mugabe. The tendency of hope espouses nationalism and anti-imperialism, but in alliance with a tyrant, while that of struggle calls for democracy, but with help from the unrepentant enemies of Africa.

The life and work of Walter Rodney teaches us that the dichotomy between hope and struggle is a false one. It is not a question of hope *or* struggle but that of hope *and* struggle. We need to combine the two, operate independently and never abandon one at the expense of the other. In Tanzania, he started off with much hope, came to realize the primacy of popular struggles, and went on to implement that in practice in his place of birth.

The irony is that those of us who theoretically critiqued him for having too much hope were not able to fully follow our own recipes for community mobilization and struggle. He was a truly dedicated revolutionary; his words were consistent with his deeds; he evolved as the concrete conditions demanded.

Let us honor the memory of this unique member of the human family by learning that lesson, and, in our collective strivings for a better world, draw the right balance between hope and struggle, between theory and practice, between specific concerns and broad transformation, between localism and internationalism, between issue oriented politics and systemic change.

As Africa remains mired in grotesque inequality, structural dependency, imperial domination and persistent poverty, consider an exaltation I think both Walter Rodney and Malcolm X would be in full agreement with:

> [L]ook at that thing the way it is. They have got a con game going on, a political con game, and you and I are in the middle. It's time for you and me to wake up and start looking at it like it is, and trying to understand it like it is; and then we can deal with it like it is (Comissiong 2012).

## CONCLUSION

A whole generation of youth, from Africa and the Caribbean, but also in Europe, America and other parts of the Third World, were inspired by Rodney and his writings, especially *HEUA*. Many were driven to activism by the exceptionally bright light he shed on the gruesome realities of the domination of Africa. He demonstrated that Africa was not poor due to innate cultural, biologic or geographic deficiencies but principally because it had been abjectly exploited for too long. In addition to its critical pedagogic value, by restoring dignity and enhancing hope, this major work became a veritable instrument for questioning the current socio-economic realities and promoting fundamental change.

History provides us means to grasp how we came to be what we are and gives a sense of purpose to life. In class societies, two distinct versions of history prevail. One promotes the vision and interests of the rulers, and the other, of the ruled. The former justifies the existent social structure; the latter queries it and seeks avenues to change it. The strong control exercised by the dominant economic class on the means of generation and promotion of ideas makes the former version inundate the public mind much of the time. In times of crisis and transformation, though, the latter version begins to surface, develop and spread (Zinn 1990).

Today the global capitalist system faces a deep crisis that manifests itself on multiple fronts. Massive economic crises, high levels of poverty, homelessness and unemployment, militarism, wars between and within nations, social instability and horrific violence, racism and xenophobia, fascistic tendencies and unbelievable extremism, public disillusionment, dysfunctional health and educational systems, voter apathy, and so on. The poor and rich nations are affected, though in varied ways.

Establishment history, in the West and elsewhere, is in a state of crisis. The traditional narrative no more exercises as strong a grip on the public mind as it did until recently. Cynicism, despair and irrational visions are on the ascendance. The US public increasingly does not buy the message that their nation is a global force for justice, rule of law and fairness. Eminent mainstream historians are worried. Seeking to counter public alienation, they are calling for a revamp of how history has been approached and presented in the past fifty years. They decry the stress on micro-level studies, gender, ethnic and post-colonial studies, short term focus, data driven strategies etc. They call for historical narratives based on unitary, society wide horizons and longer term perspectives. They ask for the reintegration of historians within the circles of decision making (Guldi and Arimtage 2014).

However rational their call may sound, ultimately it stems from a desire to protect the capitalist system. They seek to reform it and find ways to tackle the excesses like high level of inequality, mass poverty, housing crises, avaricious financial institutions, environmental catastrophe and unchecked militarism.

The peoples of the planet, the 99%, however, do not need to go in that direction. Instead of superficial reformist measures, they should strive to replace capitalism and imperialism with a just social order based on equality, internal and international cooperation, social and economic justice, peace and total disarmament. Neo-liberalism, particularly, must be exposed and banished from Africa and the planet.

Liberationist historians have a major role to play in helping that process take off. African historians, academics and activists of goodwill should think along systemic, long term lines and consider the issue of class analysis and class struggles. They need to creatively invoke the Marxist methodology. They must engage with the ideas of equality, socialism, cooperation, popular democracy, regional economic integration and planning, environmentally appropriate technology and so on in relevant ways. Instead of the micro-level, donor driven, NGO-based vision, we need independent, innovative, society level paths for progress.

Not that it will be a straightforward or easy task. As the analysis of books done earlier indicates, the bulk of the current crop of historians of Africa, of diverse historiographical persuasions, are entwined in an embrace with the neo-liberal social order. They will oppose such a move. On the continent, as well the discipline of history has suffered a major setback. In Rodney's days, the Department of History at the University of Dar es Salaam and the Historical Association of Tanzania were globally prominent in terms the volume and quality of their output on Tanzanian and African history, some which shone with methodological innovation. It was active in the improvement of history teaching in schools. Today, the quantity and quality of its publications have declined precipitously. Despite a ten-fold increase in the student population at the University, the numbers of students in history programs have remained stagnant. Most students are attracted to Business Studies, Computer Science, Communication Studies and Law. In 2016, a much-publicized event to remedy that state of affairs was organized at the University. The Historical Association of Tanzania, which had been dormant for twenty-five years, was to be revived. Yet, it was a 'donor' funded effort. One wonders how far it will go and the direction it will take (Kamagi 2016; The Citizen 2016a).

For those who will pursue an alternative path, there is a major political risk too. Adopting a Marxist stand in the academia of the Third World or the West has historically been a dangerous option, in professional and personal terms. Eminent historians have paid a steep price. In the UK, Eric Hobsbawm's career was for long thwarted by behind the scenes dirty actions of the intelligence agencies (Saunders 2015); in the US, Howard Zinn faced a life time of politically inspired barriers due to his civil rights, anti-war and social justice related writings and activism (Kirstein 2015); in Latin America, Eduardo Galeano endured years of sustained harassment, imprisonment and frequent forced exile by the US backed dictatorships (Fulton 2015); in India, the Marxist DD Kosmabi, despite his first rate output in many fields, faced career damaging moves of political origin (Kosambi 2013). Walter Rodney, the stellar Marxist historian and fighter for social justice, faced, throughout his career, a diversity of daunting hazards, and paid the ultimate price.

Yet, pursuing those avenues is essential for the liberation of Africa. More than anything else, Africa needs young activists/scholars who will write for the public and not exclusively for the academic specialist. It needs a breed of scholars who will take modern reactionary academics to task as Rodney did in his time. It needs scholars who, besides learning from his writings and methodology, will also take a fresh look at his work. They will need to rectify the factually flawed aspects of his book, and improve his approach in relation to internal class relations and class struggle. They will need to take the vastly different global reality into account. The socialist world is no more. China is a major capitalist power. The manifestations of neo-colonialism under the neo-liberal order, on the economic, political and cultural arenas, need meticulous, systemic, critical analysis.

In particular, Africa needs a four volume *People's History of Africa* that portrays the four phases of the evolution of African societies – pre-European contact, initial contact to the onset of colonial era, the colonial era and the independence period – in a systemic, Marxist perspective. That work *must* integrate the internal and external class relations and struggles with comprehensive depictions of the basic economic realities, and simultaneously link them to cultural, political and societal trends and occurrences (Depelchin 2011; Temu and Swai 1981; Therborn 2012). It should dynamically and vividly show us why things went the way they did and indicate possible ways and means out of the dire predicament Africa faces. That tome, maybe jointly produced by a group of committed intellectuals, must be supplemented with smaller derivative books written in a lively, inspiring style for popular consumption. Besides English, French and Portuguese versions, they should be available in languages like Swahili, Yoruba and Arabic. That would be a fitting legacy to our brave, departed comrade Walter Rodney.

Having said that, I confidently declare that *How Europe*

*Underdeveloped Africa* was the twentieth century's most outstanding book on the history of Africa. Its basic methodology has withstood the test of time and remains solid. It retains its relevance for understanding the African past, grasping its trajectory from the time of Independence, and importantly, for insight into distinctive future scenarios that may unfold. Let us give this intellectual giant and committed human being the credit due to him. Let us follow in his footsteps to not just interpret the world scientifically but also to join hands with the popular masses to change it effectively and for the better.

The simple words of a modern day young scholar-activist on Rodney's masterpiece sum up much of what one can say about it:

> Through the lens of scholar and academic, what is most useful about this work is its ability to enlighten and transform. ….. Through the lens of the activist and movement builder, what is most useful about this book is its ability to organize and stand in solidarity with those in the struggle to redevelop Africa (Sabrina Smiley 2010).

The question I am left with is: Considering the daunting hurdles, existential threats and mammoth tasks presently facing Africa, are its intellectuals and activists ready to take on, in the spirit of Walter Rodney, Amilcar Cabral, Chris Hani and others who valiantly struggled in days gone past, the challenges that lie ahead?

# PHOTOGRAPH FROM THE ARCHIVES

From left to right: Fatehali Hirji (my father), Walter Rodney, Karim Hirji, Munir Hirji (my brother), Joe L Kanywanyi and Haroub Othman, Dar es Salaam air- port, August 1971.

# ACKNOWLEDGEMENTS

I have been assisted by many. My heartfelt thanks go to a not-to-be-named Marxist historian who pointed out valuable sources, and gave extensive comments and advice on the initial draft. Many thanks are also due to Wendell H Marsh, Issa Shivji, Abdul Sheriff and Natasha Shivji for comments and helpful suggestions.

Three anonymous scholars selected by the Walter Rodney Foundation reviewed an earlier incarnation of this work. Patricia Rodney and Asha Rodney sent me relevant material and gave comments. A reviewer from the Daraja Press also pointed to some improvements. They all have my gratitude.

I am particularly thankful that Rosa Hirji found time from her hectic schedule to give instructive comments, meticulously edit the manuscript and assist in the selection of the title and cover design. Firoze Manji and his team at Daraja Press have earned my commendations for their efforts to expeditiously bring out this book.

Without the untiring efforts of my life partner Farida, this book would not have seen the light of the day. She has cared for me in countless way in these days of fragile health, and assisted by typing my dictation and making corrections. No words can express the gratitude I feel.

Note: A large portion of Chapter 9 is taken from a talk given at the Fifth Annual Walter Rodney Symposium held in Atlanta, Georgia, in 2013.

# MAJOR WRITINGS OF WALTER RODNEY

**Major Writings of Walter Rodney**

Rodney W (1965) Portuguese attempts at monopoly on the Upper Guinea Coast, *Journal of African History*, 6(3):307-22.

Rodney W (1966) African slavery and other forms of social oppression on the Upper Guinea Coast, 1580–1650, *Journal of African History*, 7(3):431-43.

Rodney W (1967a) *West Africa and the Atlantic Slave Trade*, Historical Association of Tanzania & East African Publishing House, Nairobi.

Rodney W (1967b) The impact of the Atlantic Slave trade in West Africa, in R Oliver (editor) *The Middle Age of African History*, Oxford University Press, Oxford, 1967.

Rodney W (1968a) Education and Tanzanian socialism, in Resnick (editor) *Tanzania: Revolution by Education*, Longmans of Tanzania, Arusha, 1968.

Rodney W (1968b) European activity and African reaction in Angola, in T Ranger (editor) *Aspects of Central African History*, Northwestern University Press, Evanston, 1968.

Rodney W (1969a) African labour under capitalism and imperialism, *Cheche*, University of Dar es Salaam, November 1969, 1:4-12.

Rodney W (1969b) Ideology of the African revolution: Paper presented at the 2nd Seminar of East and Central African Youth, *The Nationalist* (Dar es Salaam), 11 December 1969.

Rodney W (1969c) *The Groundings With My Brothers*, Bogle-L'Ouveture Publications, London.

Rodney W (1969d) Gold and slaves on the Gold Coast, *Transactions of the Historical Society of Ghana*, X, Accra.

Rodney W (1970a) *A History of the Upper Guinea Coast 1545 to 1800*, Oxford University Press, Oxford.

Rodney (1970b) The role of the university in developing Africa, Public Lecture, Makerere Students' Guild, Makerere University, Kampala, October 1970.

Rodney W (1971a) The year 1895 in southern Mozambique: African resistance to the imposition of European colonial rule, *Journal of the Historical Society of Nigeria*, 5(4):509-35.

Rodney W (1971b) George Jackson, black revolutionary, *MajiMaji*, 5:4-6.

Rodney W (1971c) Some implications of the question of disengagement from imperialism, *MajiMaji*, University of Dar es Salaam, January 1971, 1:3-8.

Rodney W (1972a) *How Europe Underdeveloped Africa* (first edition), Bogle-L'Ouveture Publications, London, and Tanzania Publishing House, Dar es Salaam.

Rodney W (1972b) Tanzanian *Ujamaa* and scientific socialism, *African Review*, 1(4):61-76. www.marxists.org/subject/africa/rodney_walter/works.

Rodney W (1973) State formation and class formation in Tanzania, *MajiMaji*, 11:25-32.

Rodney W (1974) Some implications of the question of disengagement from imperialism, in I Shivji (editor) *The Silent Class Struggle*, Tanzania Publishing House, Dar es Salaam, 1974.

Rodney W (1975a) The Guinea Coast, in R Gray (editor) *The Cambridge History of Africa, Vol. 4:c.1600—c.1790*, Cambridge University Press, London, 1975.

Rodney W (1975b) *Como a Europa subdesenvolveu a Africa*, Seara Nova, Lisboa.

Rodney W (1975c) Africa in Europe and the Americas, in R Grey (editor) *The Cambridge History of Africa*, Volume 4:c.1600—c.1790, Cambridge University Press, Cambridge, 1975.

Rodney W (1976) *World War II and the Tanzanian Economy*, Africana Research and Studies Center, Monograph Series No. 3, Cornell University, Ithaca.

Rodney W (1979a) (editor) *Guyanese Sugar Plantations in the Late Nineteenth Century: A Contemporary Description from the Argosy*, Release Publishers, Georgetown, Guyana.

Rodney W (1979b) Slavery and underdevelopment, in M Craton (editor) *Roots and Branches: Current Directions in Slave Studies*, Pergamon Press, New York, 1979.

Rodney W (1980a) Class contradictions in Tanzania, in H Othman (editor) *The State in Tanzania: Who Controls It and Whose Interests Does It Serve*, Dar es Salaam University Press, Dar es Salaam, 1980. www.marxists.org/subject/africa/rodney_walter/works.

Rodney W (1980b) The political economy of colonial Tanganyika 1890 – 1930, in MH Kaniki (editor) *Tanzania Under Colonial Rule*, Longman, London, 1980.

Rodney W (1980c) *A History of the Upper Guinea Coast 1545 to 1800* (reprint), Monthly Review Press, New York.

Rodney W (1980d) *Afrika – Die Geschiche einer Unterentwicklung*, Verlag Klauss Wagenbach, Berlin.

Rodney W (1980e) *Kofi Badau – Out of Africa*, Guyana National Lithographic Co., Georgetown.

Rodney W (1981) *A History of the Guyanese Working People, 1881 – 1905*, Heinemann Educational Books, London, and John Hopkins University Press, Baltimore.

Rodney W (1982a) *How Europe Underdeveloped Africa* (second edition), Howard University Press, Washington, DC and Bogle L'Ouverture Publications, London.

Rodney W (1982b) *de como Europa subdesarollo a Africa*, Editores Siglo XXI de Espana, Madrid.

Rodney W, Tambila K and Saop L (1983) *Migrant Labour in Tanzania During the Colonial Period*, Institute for Africa-Kunde, Hamburg.

Rodney W (1985) The colonial economy, in A Boahen (editor) *Africa Under Colonial Domination 1880 – 1935*, Heinemann and UNESCO, California, 1985.

Rodney W (1986) *Et L'Europe sous deve'loppa l'Afrique: Analyse historique et politique du sous-developpement*, Editions Caribe'ennes, Paris.

Rodney W (2011) *How Europe Underdeveloped Africa* (third edition), Pambazuka Press, Oxford; CODESRIA, Dakar; Black Classic Press, Baltimore; and Walter Rodney Foundation, Atlanta.

Rodney W (2014) *The Groundings with My Brothers* (second edition), Walter Rodney Press, East Point, GA.

*************

Notes: (i) Many of these references are extracted from the extensive bibliography in Lewis (1998). (ii) Several Walter Rodney's papers are accessible online at www.marxists.org. (iii) The website www.walterrodneyfoundation.org maintains relevant and current material about Walter Rodney.

# REFERENCES

Abdulazeez A (2014) How Africans underdeveloped Africa, *Kenya Today*, 1 March 2014, www.kenya-today.com/news/africans-under developed-africa.
Ahmad E (2001) *Terrorism: Theirs and Ours*, Seven Stories Press, New York.
Alpers EA and Fontaine PM (editors) (1982) *Walter Rodney, Revolutionary and Scholar: A Tribute*, University of California Press, Berkeley.
Alpers EA and Fontaine PM (editors) (1985) *Walter Rodney, Poetic Tributes*, Bogle-L'Ouverture Publications, London.
Amin S (1969) *The Class Struggle in Africa*, Africa Research Group, Cambridge, Massachusetts.
Amin S (1973) *Neo-Colonialism in West Africa*, Penguin, Harmondsworth.
Amin S (1978) *Accumulation on a World Scale*, Monthly Review Press, New York.
Aminzade R (2013) *Race, Nation, and Citizenship in Postcolonial Africa: The Case of Tanzania*, Cambridge University Press, New York.
Anderson D (2013) *Histories of the Hanged: The Dirty War in Kenya and the End of Empire*, WW Norton, New York.
Angell M (2005) *The Truth About the Drug Companies: How They Deceive Us and What To Do About It*, Random House, New York.
Asante MK (2007) *The History of Africa* (new edition), Routledge, New York.
Baran P (1957) *The Political Economy of Growth*, Monthly Review Press, New York.
Beckett A (2009) Has the Left blown its big chance of success? *The Guardian*. 17 August 2009, www.guardian.co.uk/politics/2009.aug/17/ left-politics-capitalism-recession.
Bernal JD (1954) *Science in History*, 4 Volumes, Watts & Co., London.
Brenan JR (2012) *Taifa: Making Nation and Race in Urban Tanzania*, Ohio University Press, Ohio.
Burgis T (2015) *The Looting Machine*, Public Affairs, New York.
Cabral A (1969) *Revolution in Guinea*, Monthly Review Press, New York.

Campbell H (1985) *Rasta and Resistance: From Marcus Garvey to Walter Rodney,* Africa World Press, Trenton, NJ.

Campbell H (1986) The impact of Walter Rodney and progressive scholars on the Dar es Salaam school, *Utafiti (Journal of the Faculty of Arts and Social Sciences),* University of Dar es Salaam, 8(2):59—77.

Chan AW, Hrobjartsson A, Haahr MT, Gotzsche PC and Altman DG (2004) Empirical evidence for selective reporting of outcomes in randomized trials: comparison of protocols and published articles, *Journal of the American Medical Association,* 291:2457—2465.

Childe G (1960) *What Happened in History,* Penguin, Middlesex.

Chung C (editor) (2013) *Walter Rodney: A Promise of a Revolution,* Monthly Review Press, New York.

Cliffe L and Saul JS (editors) (1973) *Socialism in Tanzania: A Reader,* Volumes I & II, East African Literature Bureau, Nairobi.

Cobain I (2012) *Cruel Britannia: A Secret History of Torture,* Portobello Books, London.

Cobain I (2016) *The History Thieves,* Granata, London.

Collins RO and Burns JM (2007) *A History of Sub-Saharan Africa,* Cambridge University Press, Cambridge, UK.

Comissiong S (2012) Dear Black America: It's past time to wake up, *Black Agenda Report,* 18 December 2012. http://www.blackagendareport.com/content/dear-black-america-its-past-time-wake

Coulson A (editor) (1979) *African Socialism in Practice: The Tanzanian Experience,* Spokesman, Nottingham.

Coulson A (2014) *Tanzania: A Political Economy* (second edition), Oxford University Press, Oxford.

Creighton A (2000) The Walter Rodney factor in West Indian literature, *Stabroek News,* 18 June 2000, www.guyanacaribbeanpolitics.com/wpa/Rodney_literature.html.

D'Amato P (2006) *The Meaning of Marxism,* Haymarket Books, Chicago.

Danaher K (1994) *50 Years Is Enough: The Case Against the World Bank and the International Monetary Fund,* South End Press, Brooklyn, MA.

Davidson B (1964) *Which Way Africa?* Penguin, Harmondsworth.

Davidson B (1966) *Africa: History of a Continent,* Macmillan, New York.

DeAngelis CD (2000) Conflict of interest and the public trust (editorial), *Journal of the American Medical Association,* 284:2237-38.

DeAngelis CD (2006) The influence of money on medical science (editorial), *Journal of the American Medical Association,* 296:E1–E3, doi:10.1001/jama.296.8.jed60051.

Deardon N (2015) Is development becoming a toxic term? *Pambazuka News,* Issue 711, 27 January 2015, pmbazuka.org/en/category/comment/93811.

Depelchin J (2011) *Reclaiming African History,* Pambazuka Press, Oxford.

Diop CA (1974) *The African Origins of Western Civilization*, Lawrence Hill Books, Chicago.
Drake P and Lalljie R (2009) (editors) *Walter Rodney: His Last Days and Campaigns*, R Ferdinand-Lalljie Publishers, London.
Dunbar-Ortiz R (2014) *An Indigenous Peoples' History of the United States*, Beacon Press, Boston.
Editor (2015) Africa/Global: Capital flows in context, *AfricaFocus Bulletin*, 2 June 2015, www.africafocus.org/docs15/tax1506b.php #sthash.jRDsddnh.dpuf.
Editorial (2004) Depressing research, *The Lancet*, 363:1335.
Editorial (2006) Unravelling industry bias in clinical trials, *Pain*, 121:175-6.
Elkins C (2005) *Imperial Reckoning: The Untold Story of Britain's Gulag in Kenya*, Holt, New York.
Engles F (2010) *The Origin of the Family, Private Property and the State*, Penguin Classics, London.
Engels F (1890) Letter to J Bloch, 21 September 1890, London, www.marxist.com/historical-materialism-study-guide.htm.
Epstein H (2015) Who's afraid of African democracy, *Common Dreams*, 25 May 2015, www.commondreams.org.
Fanon F (1963) *The Wretched of the Earth*, Grove Press, New York.
Ford G (2012) Commentaries and Blogs, www.blackagendareport.com.
Fouere MA (editor) (2015) *Remembering Nyerere in Tanzania: History, Memory, Legacy*, Mkuki na Nyota, Dar es Salaam.
Foster JB (2006) *Naked Imperialism: The US Pursuit of Global Dominance*, Monthly Review Press, New York.
Frank AG (1967) *Capitalism and Underdevelopment in Latin America*, Monthly Review Press, New York.
Frank AG (1969) *Latin America: Underdevelopment or Revolution*, Monthly Review Press, New York.
Freire P (1968;2000) *Pedagogy of the Oppressed*, Bloomsbury Academic, New York.
Freund B (1998) *The Making of Contemporary Africa: The Development of African Society since 1800* (second edition), Palgrave Macmillan, UK.
Fulton D (2015) Writer Eduardo Galeano, voice of Latin America's Left, dead at 74, *Common Dreams*, 13 April 2015, http://www.commondreams.org/news/2015/04/13/writer-eduardo-galeano-voice-latin-americas-left-dead-74
Gabriehu A (2007) *Dangerous Times: The Assassination of Dr. Walter Rodney* (second edition), Ghebbi Books, Brooklyn, NY.
Galeano E (1974; 2009) *Open Veins of Latin America: Five Centuries of Pillage of a Continent* (new edition), Serpents Tail, New York.
Gilbert ET and Reynolds JT (2011) *Africa in World History* (third edition), Pearson, UK.

Grandin G (2011) *The Last Colonial Massacre: Latin America in the Cold War* (updated edition), University of Chicago Press, Chcago.

Guha R (2013) DD Kosambi's teachings on the importance of the superstructure in history, in M Kosambi (editor) (2013), p 198-227.

Guldi J and Armitage D (2014) *The History Manifesto*, Cambridge University Press, Cambridge (UK).

Hickel J (2014) Exposing the great 'poverty reduction scandal', *Common Dreams*, 22 August 2014, www.commondreams.org.

Hirji KF (1973) School education and underdevelopment in Tanzania, *MajiMaji*, No. 12:1–23.

Hirji KF (2009) No Short-Cut in Assessing Trial Quality: A Case Study, *Trials*, 10:1 (45 pages with additional files), (www.trialsjournal.com) (Highly accessed paper with editorial commentary: Gotzsche (2009) *Trials*, 10:2)

Hirji KF (2011) *Cheche: Reminiscences of a Radical Magazine*, Mkuki na Nyota, Dar es Salaam.

Hirji KF and Premji Z (2011) Pre-referral rectal Artesunate in severe malaria: A flawed trial, *Trials*, 12:188, www.trialsjournal.com/content/12/1/188.

Hirji KF (2013) Hope and struggle: Walter Rodney as I knew him, Presentation at the Fifth Annual Walter Rodney Symposium, Walter Rodney Foundation, Atlanta, Georgia, 3 March 2013, *Chemchemi* (University of Dar es Salaam), 6:12—18.

Hirji KF (2014a) *Growing Up With Tanzania: Memory, Musings and Maths*, Mkuki na Nyota, Dar es Salaam.

Hirji KF (2014b) Beating the drum on one side: Confusing the people on both sides, *Awaaz Magazine*, 11(3):36–41, www.awaazmagazine.com.

Hochschild A (1999) *King Leopold's Ghost: A Story of Greed, Terror, and Heroism in Colonial Africa*, Houghton Mifflin, New York

Iliffe J (2007) *Africans: The History of a Continent* (second edition, African Studies), Cambridge University Press, Cambridge, UK.

Ivaska A (2011) *Cultured States: Youth, Gender, and Modern Style in 1960s Dar es Salaam*, Duke University Press, Durham and London.

Jack I (2016) *The History Thieves* by Ian Cobain review – how Britain covered up its imperial crimes, *The Guardian*, 6 October 2016, www.theguardian.com/books/2016/oct/06.

Jalee P (1970) *The Pillage of the Third World*, Monthly Review Press, New York.

James CLR (1973) Reflections on Pan-Africanism. Speech given on 20 November 1973, www.marxists.org/archive/james-clr/works.

James CLR (1981) Walter Rodney and the question of power, *Race Today*, Talk given on 30 January 1981, www.marxists.org/archive/james-clr/works.

James CLR (1993) *Beyond a Boundary* (reprint edition), Duke University Press, Durham.

Kamagi D (2016) More History programmes to be offered at UDSM, *The Citizen* (Tanzania), 21 November 2016.

Kaniki MHY (editor) (1980) *Tanzania Under Colonial Rule*, Longman Group, United Kingdom.

Kassirer J (2000) Financial indigestion, *Journal of the American Medical Association*, 284:2156-7.

Kirstein PN (2015) Review essay on Howard Zinn, *Logos: A Journal of Modern Society and Culture*, logosjournal.com/2015/review-essay-on-howard-zinn/

Klein N (2008) *The Shock Doctrine: The Rise of Disaster Capitalism*, Picador, London.

Kolumbia L (2016) Government warns it will close more universities, *The Citizen* (Tanzania), 26 November 2016.

Kosambi DD (1956;1975) *An Introduction to the Study of Indian History* (second edition), Popular Prakashan Ltd, India.

Kosambi M (editor) (2013) *Unsettling the Past: Unknown Aspects and Scholarly Assessments of DD Kosambi*, Permanent Black, India.

Kwayana E (2013) *Walter Rodney: His Last Days and Campaigns*, R Ferdinand-Lalljie Publishers, UK.

Kwayana E (2014) Walter Rodney: Why the Chinese want to read him, *Pambazuka News*, Issue 660, 8 January 2014, pambazuka.org/en/category/comment/90083.

Lamtey G (2016) Project to create jobs for youth launched, *The Citizen* (Tanzania), 26 November 2016.

Laumann D (2012) *Colonial Africa: 1884-1994* (*African World Histories*), Oxford University Press, Oxford.

Lawi J (2016) Hope in Obama's youth initiative in Tanzania, *The Guardian* (Tanzania), 17 November 2016.

Lenin VI (1916;1939) *Imperialism: The Highest Stage of Capitalism*, International Publishers, Moscow.

Lewis RC (1998) *Walter Rodney's Intellectual and Political Thought*, Wayne State University Press, Barbados and Detroit.

Lewis S (2010) Neoliberalism, conflict of interest, and the governance of health research in Canada, *Open Medicine*, 1(1):28-30, www.openmedicine.ca.

Lindqvist S (1997) *"Exterminate All the Brutes": One Man's Odyssey into the Heart of Darkness and the Origins of European Genocide*, The New Press, New York.

Magdoff H (2003) *Imperialism Without Colonies*, Monthly Review Press, New York.

Mamdani M (1976) *Politics and Class Formation in Uganda*, Monthly Review Press, New York.

Mamdani M (1984) *Imperialism and Fascism in Uganda*, Africa World Press, New York.

Mamdani M (2005) *Good Muslim, Bad Muslim: America, the Cold War and the Roots of Terror*, Harmony, New York.

Mamdani M (2008a) Why Africans fight, *The East African*, 19 December 2008.

Mamdani M (2008b) Amnesty for Africa's serial killers, *The East African*, 27 December 2008.

Mamdani M (2011) An African reflection on Tahrir Square, *The East African*, 16 May 2011.

Mamdani M (2012) *Define and Rule: Native as Political Identity (The WEB Du Bois Lectures)*, Harvard University Press, Cambridge, MA.

Maoulidi S (2009) Racial and religious tolerance in Nyerere's political thought and practice, *Pambazuka News*, Issue No 452, 13 October 2009, www.pambazukanews.org

Mapolu H (editor) (1979) *Workers and Management in Tanzania*, Tanzania Publishing House, Dar es Salaam.

Mapolu H (1986) The state and the peasantry, in IG Shivji (editor) (1986):107–131.

Mapolu H (1990) Tanzania: Imperialism, the state and the peasantry, In HA Amara and B Founou-Tchuigoua (editors) *African Agriculture: The Critical Choices*, Zed Books, London, Chapter 8.

Marable M (1999) *How Capitalism Underdeveloped Black America: Problems in Race, Political Economy, and Society*, South End Press Classics Series, Boston, MA.

Mathur P (2013) Book Review: *Define and Rule: Native as a Political Identity* by Mahmood Mamdani, *Asia Times*, 2 August 2013.

Mayer M (2005) When clinical trials are compromised: A perspective from a patient advocate, *PLoS Medicine*, 2:e358.

Mazanza M (2016) 'Mzungu kicha' of Bongo Star Search fame roots for Kiswahili, *The Guardian* (Tanzania), 15 November 2016.

Mbilinyi M (1979) The Arusha Declaration and Education for Self-Reliance, In A Coulson (editor) (1979) *African Socialism in Practice: The Tanzanian Experience*, Spokesman, Nottingham.

McCauley L (2015) Exploitation of a higher kind: How the G7 is fuelling corporate dominion of Africa, *Common Dreams*, 3 June 2015, www.commondreams.org.

Mills G (2011) *Why Africa is Poor and What Africans Can Do About It*, Penguin Global, New York and London.

Mishambi GT (1977) The mystification of African history: a critique of *How Europe Underdeveloped Africa*, *Utafiti* (University of Dar es Salaam), 2(2):201-28.

Moore TJ (1995) *Deadly Medicine: Why Tens of Thousands of Patients Died in America's Worst Drug Disaster*, Simon & Shuster, New York.

Mukerjee M (2011) *Churchill's Secret War: The British Empire and the Ravaging of India during World War II*, Basic Books, New York.

Nkrumah K (1966) *Neo-Colonialism: The Last Stage of Imperialism*, International Publishers, London.

Nyerere JK (1967) Education for Self-Reliance, In JK Nyerere (1968) *Freedom and Socialism: A Selection of Writings and Speeches, 1965—1967*, Oxford University Press, Dar es Salaam and Oxford.

Oliver R and Fage JD (1962;1990) *A Short History of Africa* (sixth edition), Penguin Books, Harmondsworth.

Othman H (editor) (1980) *The State in Tanzania: Who Controls It and Whose Interests Does It Serve?* Dar es Salaam University Press, Dar es Salaam.

Othman H (2005) Walter Rodney – A revolutionary intellectual, In SY Othman (editor) (2014), pp 299—302.

Othman SY (editor) (2014) *Yes, in My Life Time: Selected Works of Haroub Othman*, Mkuki na Nyota & CODESRIA, Dar es Salaam & Dakar.

Perkins J (2005) *Confessions of an Economic Hit Man*, Plume, New York.

Pradella L and Marois T (2015) (editors) *Polarising Development: Alternatives to Neoliberalism and the Crisis*, Pluto Press, London.

Prashad V (2007) *The Darker Nations: A People's History of the Third World*, The New Press, New York.

Reader J (1999) *Africa: A Biography of the Continent*, Vintage, New York.

Reid RJ (2012) *A History of Modern Africa: 1800 to the Present* (second edition), Wiley-Blackwell, New York.

Resnick IN (editor) (1968) *Tanzania: Revolution by Education*, Longmans of Tanzania Limited, Arusha.

Rostow WW (1960) *The Stages of Economic Growth: A Non-Communist Manifesto*, Cambridge University Press, Cambridge.

Rweyemamu JF (1973) *Underdevelopment and Industrialization in Tanzania: A Study of Perverse Capitalist Industrial Development*, Oxford University Press, Nairobi.

Said M (2014) Tanzania: A nation without heroes, *Awaaz Magazine*, 11(3):32–35, www.awaazmagazine.com.

Salkey A (1974) *Joey Tyson*, Bogle-L'Ouverture Publications, London.

Saul JS (1971) Who is the Immediate Enemy? *MajiMaji*, No. 1:9-15.

Saunders FS (2015) Stuck on the flypaper, *London Review of Books*, 37(07), www.lrb.co.uk/v37/n07/frances-stonorsaunders/stuck-on-the-flypaper.

Scott JW (2015) The new thought police, *The Nation*, 15 April 2015, www.the nation.com/article/204481/new-thought-police.

Sharife K (2009) Tanzania's pot of gold: Not much revenue at the end of the rainbow, *Pambazuka News*, 1 October 2009, Issue 450, www.pambazuka.org/en/category/features/59142.

Shaxson N (2012) *Treasure Islands: Tax Havens and the Men Who Stole the World*, Vintage Books, London.
Shillington K (2012) *History of Africa* (third edition), Palgrave-MacMillan, New York.
Shivji IG (1970) The Silent Class Struggle, *Cheche* No 3 (University of Dar es Salaam), September 1970, Special Issue.
Shivji IG (1973) *Tanzania: The Silent Class Struggle: With Commentaries by Walter Rodney, John Saul and Thomas Szentes*, Zeni Press, UK.
Shivji IG (1976) *Class Struggles in Tanzania*, Heinemann, London.
Shivji IG (editor) (1987) *State and the Working People in Tanzania*, CODESRIA Book Series, Dakar.
Shivji IG (1993) *Intellectuals at the Hill: Essays and Talks 1960—1993*, Dar es Salaam University Press, Dar es Salaam.
Shivji IG (2012) Remembering Walter Rodney, *Monthly Review*, 64(7).
Smiley S (2010) Book Review: How Europe Underdeveloped Africa, *Mosaic African Studies E-Journal* (Howard University Department of History), 1(1).
Smulewitz-Zucker G and Thompson AJ (2015) The treason of intellectual radicalism and the collapse of leftist politics, *Logos*, logosjournal.com/2015/thompson-zucker/.
Swai B (1981) Rodney on scholarship and activism – Part 1, *Journal of African Marxists*, Issue 1: 31—43.
Swai B (1982) Rodney on scholarship and activism – Part 2, *Journal of African Marxists*, Issue 2: 38—52.
TANU (1967) *The Arusha Declaration and TANU's Policy of Socialism and Self-Reliance*, TANU Publicity Section, Dar es Salaam.
TANU (1971) *Mwongozo: TANU Guidelines*, National Printing Company, Dar es Salaam.
TANU Youth League (1980) *Special Issue on Walter Rodney, MajiMaji*, University of Dar es Salaam, No. 43.
Temu AJ and Swai B (1981) *Historians and History: Africanist History Examined*, Zed Press, London.
Thapar R (2013) The contribution of DD Kosambi to Indology, in M Kosambi (editor) (2013), pp 175—197.
Traboulsi F (2012) The Left in time of revolution. *Socialist Project E-Bulletin*, No 727, 11 November 2012, http://therealnews.com/t2/component/content/article/187-more-blog-posts-from-fawwaz-traboulsi/1318-the-left-in-time-of-revolution
The Citizen (2016a) Dar varsity revives History Association, *The Citizen* (Tanzania), 18 November 2016.
The Citizen (2016b) Researchers identify Africa's tallest tree on Mt Kilimanjaro, *The Citizen* (Tanzania), 29 November 2016.
Therborn G (2012) Class in the 21st Century, *New Left* Review, 78:5

https://newleftreview.org/II/78/goran-therborn-class-in-the-21st-century

Tungaraza E (2016) Preparing students for the future, *The Citizen* (Tanzania), 2 November 2016.

Turse N (2015) The US military's battlefield of tomorrow, *Common Dreams*, 15 April 2015, www.commondreams.org/views/ 2015/04/15/ us-militarys-battlefield-tomorrow.

Vine D (2015) *Base Nation: How US Military Bases Abroad Harm America and the World*, Metropolitan Books, New York.

Von Freyhold M (1979) *Ujamaa Villages in Tanzania: Analysis of a Social Experiment*, Monthly Review Press, New York.

Wamba dia Wamba (1980) Walter Rodney and the role of the revolutionary intellectual in the neo-colonial countries, in TANU Youth League (1980).

Ward P and Kirschvink J (2015) *A New History of Life*, Bloomsbury Press, New York.

Westmas N (2012) Forty years of *How Europe Underdeveloped Africa*, *Stabroek News*, 10 June 2012.

Wikipedia (2014) Walter Rodney, *Wikipedia*, http://en/wikipedia.org/wiki/ Walter_Rodney?oldid=62231619.

Wolf E (2014) *Pillaging the World*, Tectum Verlag, Berlin.

Wright DR and Reilly K (2010) *The World and a Very Small Place in Africa: The History of Globalization in Numi, the Gambia*, ME Sharp Inc., New York.

X Malcolm (1965) *The Autobiography of Malcolm X*, Grove Press, New York.

Zinn H (1980) *A People's History of the United States*, Harper & Row, New York.

Zinn H (1990) *The Politics of History* (second edition), University of Illinois Press, Illinois.

## MAIN QUOTATIONS

The Gandhi exchange on Western civilization appears in many places. But reliable evidence as to when and where it occurred is not available. The Madeline Albright quotes are extracted from https://williamblum.org/essays.

# ABOUT THE AUTHOR

**Karim F Hirji** is a retired Professor of Medical Statistics and a Fellow of the Tanzania Academy of Sciences. A recognized authority on statistical analysis of small sample discrete data, the author of the only book on the subject, he received the Snedecor Prize for Best Publication in Biometry from the American Statistical Association and International Biometrics Society for the year 1989. He has published many papers in the areas of statistical methodology, applied biomedical research, the history and practice of education in Tanzania, and written numerous essays on varied topics for the mass media and popular magazines.

He is the author of *Exact Analysis of Discrete Data* (Chapman and Hall/CRC Press, Boca Raton, 2005), *Statistics in the Media: Learning from Practice*, (Media Council of Tanzania, Dar es Salaam, 2012) and *Growing Up With Tanzania: Memories, Musings and Maths* (Mkuki na Nyota Publishers, Dar es Salaam, 2014). He also edited and is the main author of *Cheche: Reminiscences of a Radical Magazine*, (Mkuki na Nyota Publishers, Dar es Salaam, 2011).

He resides in Dar es Salaam, Tanzania, and may be contacted at kfhirji@aol.com.

www.ingramcontent.com/pod-product-compliance
Lightning Source LLC
Chambersburg PA
CBHW050541300426
44113CB00012B/2207